Negotiating in the Public Eye

The Impact of the Press on the Intermediate-Range Nuclear Force Negotiations

Negotiating
in the Public Eye

*The Impact of the Press on
the Intermediate-Range
Nuclear Force Negotiations*

Marc A. Genest

Stanford University Press, Stanford, California 1995

Stanford University Press
Stanford, California
© 1995 by the Board of Trustees of the
Leland Stanford Junior University
Printed in the United States of America

CIP data appear at the end of the book

Stanford University Press publications are distributed
exclusively by Stanford University Press within
the United States, Canada, and Mexico;
they are distributed exclusively by Cambridge University
Press throughout the rest of the world.

For my loving wife, Marcy

Acknowledgments

Many times in the course of writing this book, I was reminded that a work of this size and complexity is not produced in a vacuum or by a single person toiling in isolation. Indeed, the financial, editorial, and emotional burdens associated with the work were shared by several outstanding organizations and individuals.

I would like to thank the United States Institute of Peace for awarding me a Peace Scholar Grant, which allowed me to complete much of the research for this book. Equally, I extend my appreciation to the Department of State's Arms Control and Disarmament Agency for its award and financial assistance. The views and opinions expressed in this work are not those of the United States government.

I am also grateful to the people at Stanford University Press for their editorial assistance and commitment to this project. In particular, I wish to thank Muriel Bell for her support in bringing this manuscript to press.

This book would be only a shadow of what it is today were it not for the input and guidance of Michael Robinson, to whom I acknowledge my boundless gratitude. From the beginning of the project to its successful conclusion, Michael's intelligence, insights, and wit added to and shaped both this book and me. He gave unselfishly of his time and expertise.

For their helpful comments, encouragement, and criticism I also wish to thank Clyde Wilcox, Robert Lieber, William O'Brien, Mark Lagon, and Susan Lagon. All were a great help to me in completing this project.

From beginning to end, one constant in my life was my wife, Marcy. She was always there as a calm voice of reason, and a skilled—not to mention patient—graphic designer. Through ups and downs, her giving nature, outstanding gourmet cuisine, and firm belief in both me and this project made it all possible.

M.A.G.

Contents

Figures

Negotiating in the Public Eye

*The Impact of the Press on
the Intermediate-Range
Nuclear Force Negotiations*

CHAPTER I

Introduction

> Arms control is ninety percent public relations. . . .
> It is a public relations war—a propaganda war. . . .
> And the Reagan administration understood this.
>
> I myself can never forget and never ignore the fact
> that you're dealing with a medium that can cut
> you up. To that extent, you better be wary and
> understand it [the press] as a potential adversary.
> I never forget that.

On November 18, 1981, in a speech at the
National Press Club in Washington, D.C., President Ronald
Reagan unveiled a new proposal to eliminate U.S. and Soviet
intermediate-range nuclear forces (INF) in Europe.[1] This proposal, labeled the "zero option," was an offer to cancel planned
deployment of American missiles if the Soviets would disman-
tle their own medium-range forces already in place. It was
the first major policy move by the Reagan administration on
INF.

It was no accident that the zero option not only made its de-
but at the National Press Club but was also carried on television
at 10 A.M. The U.S. International Communication Agency—
now the U.S. Information Agency (USIA)—arranged for live sat-
ellite transmission of the speech to Western Europe. At that
time Europeans would just be arriving home from work and
turning on the news so this strategy would likely ensure the
largest audience possible.[2]

From the outset, INF was characterized by public diplomacy.
The zero option was not presented to the Soviet negotiating
team in Geneva until December 11, 1981. Apparently, it was
the eye of the media that the Reagan administration wanted to

and did capture by carefully planning where the announcement would be given, when it would be delivered, and how it would be covered by the press. The zero option and its carefully crafted presentation represented the new administration's first salvo in the propaganda war that characterized both INF policymaking and negotiations.

The Reagan government understood the importance of the media in the politics of INF, which became the most public of all "secret" arms control negotiations ever conducted. This new strategy of public diplomacy dramatically expanded the importance, role, and, probably, influence of the media. The press, both electronic and print, was the medium through which and the forum in which the United States and the Soviet Union waged their arms control battles on INF.

Goals

Using INF policymaking and negotiations as a case study, this book examines the role and impact of the press. The goal is to clear up some of the confusion about press behavior with regard to arms control specifically and U.S. foreign policy more broadly. In addition, I will look at the nature of the relationship between the media, the government, and the public.

The intent in exploring these issues was not to establish the absolute correctness of a particular theory on press behavior across the board but, rather, to determine which model of the press best describes the media's behavior and, as a consequence, their potential impact.

Books have been written about the power and role (or lack thereof) of the press with respect to various political domains. Material is much more limited, however, in the research field of the media and foreign policy, particularly arms control. There is no comprehensive study of press behavior in this area that uses both quantitative data and qualitative research. Previous works have been based on fairly narrow or impressionistic evidence—data from either the electronic or the print press or interviews alone, with no corroborating quantitative analysis.

Methods

This book combines these two forms of analysis, incorporating data from both television and print news coverage along with interviews of journalists and officials involved in the INF issue. This combination of quantitative analysis and qualitative insight allows for comprehensive conclusions about press behavior and influence on INF.

The book is divided into two parts along these quantitative-qualitative lines. As a prelude, the review of related literature establishes the theoretical structure for looking at press behavior, which is then used as a framework for the study. Two of the theories—agenda-setting and agenda-building—were drawn from existing scholarly works. The third, called here agenda-reflecting, represents a model that has not yet been formally labeled, although its tenets have a significant following among scholars and experts.

These theories establish the guidelines for examining the data in the first part of the book, the content of both television and print news coverage of INF from 1981 through 1987. The analysis of the coverage answers two of the three questions asked in the study to help define press behavior. First, where did the press get information on INF? Answers to this question help to determine the relative dependence or independence of the press on official government sources of information. The more independent the press's sources—that is, the more they originate outside government—the more we can posit that the press is empowered or independent.

The second question asks how the press then presents that information to the public: what was the tone of press coverage on INF? Again, the data from both networks and newspapers in Part I provide evidence about the independence of the press in this regard. That is, news coverage inherently critical or supportive of administration policy might indicate that the press had an alternative political agenda.

Where the press got information and how it presented that information to the public are the two primary questions addressed in the content analysis. The quantitative analysis, presented in Part I of the book, was believed to be the best way to answer these two questions.

The third question—what impact did this press coverage have on policymaking and the negotiations—is more subjective. The second part of the book considers the question of the impact and behavior of the press with regard to INF.

The methodology in Part II shifts from quantitative to qualitative evidence on press behavior—interviews with journalists and government officials. Evidence from these interviews is designed to complement and complete the investigation that began with the content analysis by providing vital insights, first, into journalists' view of their own position during INF and how they evaluate their role in the process and, second, what effect officials thought the media coverage and the press had on their ability to make policy and negotiate an agreement. Using interviews with journalists and officials provides some balance between the opinions of those who were making—or trying to make—the news and those who were reporting it.

But what about those who were presumably reading or watching the news—the public? Some general figures on public opinion are discussed, but a detailed investigation of trends over the 1981–87 period was left to a separate study. For the purposes of this book, officials' perceptions of public opinion and its impact, in combination with some general statistics, proved sufficient for drawing conclusions about press behavior and impact.

A Map for Readers

Dividing the book into two parts is also designed to make it easier for individual readers to tailor what they read to their own specific interests. The first chapter in Part I provides an overview of material in the field of press behavior and impact and a description of the three theoretical models that are used throughout. For those readers who are looking for a solid grounding in the theoretical principles used in the study, Chapter 2 is recommended.

Chapters 3 and 4 focus on network coverage and newspaper

coverage, respectively, and apply the three models of press behavior to the data. Because of the size of the data base, these chapters have been structured and presented as simply as possible for the sake of clarity. Readers interested in quantitative methods would probably find Chapters 3 and 4 of particular interest.

Chapters 5 and 6 in Part II focus on qualitative evidence of press behavior, based on interviews with reporters and officials involved with INF. The beginning of each chapter addresses whether and to what degree the interviewees corroborated findings from the content analysis on the "where" and "how" questions of news coverage. Though this method might appear a bit redundant, I have done it to satisfy those readers who may not have been interested in or persuaded by the quantitative material presented in Chapters 3 and 4.

The second part of the book is primarily devoted to qualitative evidence addressing the question of press impact. Impact, per se, is a subjective issue that is difficult to answer quantitatively. I believed the best way to evaluate impact was to talk with those people who were involved with INF from both sides—journalists and officials. Government officials, in particular, had to deal with the press and press coverage on a regular basis and were in a good position to judge the impact of the media on policymaking and the negotiations.

The conclusion to the book consists of simply that—conclusions. They are not presented as final or unalterable truths, but rather as an attempt to identify and clarify the role of the press in the arms control negotiation process. This case study might also offer some insight into the nature of the overall relationship between the press, the government, and the public.

A Brief History of INF

Before beginning this odyssey through the currents of media impact, it will be useful to give a brief history of the events leading up to the INF Treaty of December 1987. Though a daily chronology was not considered necessary, an overview of major events should be helpful.

The Soviet Union first deployed intermediate-range nuclear missiles in its western republics late in 1976 and into early 1977. To compensate for this deployment, the North Atlantic Treaty Organization (NATO) announced a "dual-track" strategy in December 1979. The United States would deploy its own intermediate-range forces in Europe while simultaneously negotiating with the Soviets for the removal of this class of missile from both sides.

The first major policy initiative in this area came when President Reagan presented his zero option proposal on November 18, 1981. The plan offered to cancel U.S. deployments in Europe, scheduled for 1983, in exchange for the removal of Soviet INF missiles. Twelve days later, on November 30, 1981, negotiations between the United States and the Soviet Union on INF began in Geneva, Switzerland, and the zero option was presented to the Soviet delegation on December 11, 1981, though it was not accepted.

Active discussion of INF, in both governmental and nongovernmental spheres, continued through 1982. In June, the United Nations opened a special session on nuclear disarmament. One of several peaks in the volume of press coverage devoted to INF for 1982 occurred during this UN conference.

The "walk in the woods" compromise of July 16, 1982, received relatively little coverage by the press at the time, with the exception of the *Chicago Tribune*. During a stroll through the woods behind the Soviet mission in Geneva, U.S. negotiator for INF, Paul Nitze, and his Soviet counterpart, Yuli Kvitsinsky, reached an unofficial agreement that would have allowed each side to retain a specific, reduced number of missiles.[3] Both governments, however, subsequently rejected this compromise.

Negotiations on INF continued in Geneva, and in December 1982, Soviet leader Yuri Andropov offered to reduce Soviet intermediate-range missiles to the combined level of French and British forces, if the United States would abandon plans for deployment. Andropov stated that deployment would not only jeopardize negotiations on INF but also would hurt prospects for limiting other classes of nuclear weapons.

In March 1983, the United States responded with its own

proposal, offering to restrict deployment if the Soviets would reduce their own INF to an equal number. Moscow rejected the offer, and, on November 23, 1983, the first American Pershing II missiles arrived in Europe. On the same day, the Soviet delegation walked out of the negotiations in Geneva as a protest and refused to commit to a date for resumption of the talks.

Over the next year, the Soviets launched an intensive media campaign against the U.S. deployment, rejecting U.S. offers to resume talks while American missiles were being installed in Western Europe. Indeed, it was not until Secretary of State George Shultz and Foreign Minister Andrei Gromyko met in Geneva on January 7–8, 1985, that the United States and the Soviet Union agreed to resume their negotiations. In March 1985, both countries returned to Geneva, and negotiations began again.

In October 1985, Soviet general secretary Mikhail Gorbachev proposed that each side cut INF by 50 percent. In November the United States countered with a plan of its own, offering specific limits on intermediate-range missiles commensurate with the number that would already be deployed in Western Europe by the end of 1985.

Neither proposal was accepted by the other side, but General Secretary Gorbachev and President Reagan did meet in Geneva on November 19, 1985. Both men agreed to continue to seek an agreement that would limit or reduce INF in Europe.

The next meeting between Reagan and Gorbachev took place in Reykjavik, Iceland, on October 11–12, 1986. There, they agreed in principle to limit each side to 100 INF warheads, deployed outside of continental Europe. Though Gorbachev dropped the demand that French and British forces be included in the total, he insisted that any agreement on INF be tied to both strategic and space weapons. In the postsummit aftermath, each side backed away from the conditions of the agreement at Reykjavik.

It was not until 1987 that the two nations began to come together on conditions for an agreement. On February 28, 1987, Gorbachev shifted his position and announced Moscow's willingness to reach an agreement on INF that was not linked to either strategic or space weapons. At a meeting between Secretary Shultz and Soviet foreign minister Edward Shevardnadze in Moscow on April 12–15, 1987, the Soviets proposed complete elimination of shorter-range INF missiles. Though the United States had no missiles of this class, the Soviets had approximately 100.

Only three months later, on July 22, 1987, Gorbachev accepted the double zero plan, proposing the elimination of all INF missiles. Details of the agreement, including verification procedures, were worked out over the next four months. The INF Treaty between the United States and the Soviet Union was signed by President Reagan and General Secretary Gorbachev on December 8, 1987, in Washington, D.C.

A Case Study in Press Behavior

Both policy and events leading up to the signing of the INF Treaty received tremendous scrutiny by the media. The INF issue was unique in that no other treaty, agreement, negotiations, or arms control policy had received such concentrated press attention. Over the seven-year period, this coverage amounted to over 4,800 *New York Times* and *Washington Post* articles and more than 2,000 minutes of time during the evening news broadcasts of the major networks—ABC, CBS, and NBC.

The amount of coverage—both time and articles—devoted to INF can be viewed as a new threshold in press behavior and its potential impact on arms control and American foreign policy. Never before had the media played such an integral role in the diplomatic process. For this reason, INF was selected as a case study. It is hoped that this example will provide some useful insights into how the press might interact with or react to future foreign policy issues.

The goal of this book is to take a look at this public diplomacy and perform a systematic examination of the role of the press in the arms control process. The study relies on a content analysis of newspaper and television reports on INF, as well as interviews with government officials and journalists. The foray begins with an overview of what scholars and other experts have said about the press and press behavior.

PART I

The Content Analysis

CHAPTER 2

Theories of Press Behavior

You should always believe all you read in the
newspapers, as this makes them more interesting.
— Rose Macauley

The question of the power of the press and its
ability to influence the course of U.S. arms control negotiations, specifically, and American foreign policy, generally, has
drawn little scholarly attention, despite increasingly intense
network and newspaper coverage of arms control talks during
the last decade. I suggest that, as an elite interest group, the
media had the power to influence both policymaking and the
political agenda.

To assess the press's impact, however, first a framework for
the analysis must be established. This chapter describes three
schools of thought on the relationship between the press, the
government, and the public. Each of the schools, or theories,
emphasizes different strengths in the interaction of media, government, and public opinion. It is important to develop these
theories fully to see how they apply to the research presented
later in the study.

Few scholarly works have given more than cursory attention
to the relationship between U.S. arms control negotiations and
the coverage of these events by the media. Among these publications, only a handful of articles have dealt specifically with
the role of the press in the negotiating process itself.

In the absence of scholarly work focusing on this issue, this
discussion uses a broader context for investigation. General
literature on the impact of the media on public opinion and the
relationship between the press and the government provides
data and basic tenets of interaction. With these tools, it is

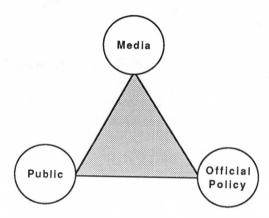

Fig. 1. Government Behavior, Press Behavior, and Public Behavior Triangle

possible to develop a more specific theoretical framework to analyze the role of the media in the making of foreign policy.

Three elements make up the input into the press-policy equation in this framework. Government behavior, press behavior, and public behavior (or response) are like three points of a triangle (see Figure 1). Differences and fluctuations in the legs (relationships) connecting these points determine the dimension and characteristics of the triangle.

Schools of thought evolve through various premises and notions about how the government, press, and public interact. The changing nature of this relationship results in the different theories (or schools of thought) described here.

For this study, three general schools of thought are used to describe the role the press might play in policymaking: agenda-setting, agenda-building, and agenda-reflecting. Each of these schools supports a theory regarding the relationship and role of the media in making foreign policy. They range from portraying the media as a major force in policymaking to viewing the press as mainly a transmitter of the government's agenda.

These schools of thought are discussed here in descending order. That is, we begin with the agenda-setting school, which credits the media with having significant influence. We move then to the agenda-building school and, finally, to the school developed for this study, labeled agenda-reflecting.

Agenda-Setting

The agenda-setting theory is most frequently attributed to Bernard Cohen, who defined the theory succinctly: "It [the press] may not be successful much of the time in telling people what to think, but it is stunningly successful in telling its readers what to think about."[1] In other words, the media define important issues that should concern the public and policy alternatives that are available. Cohen's theory, however, was a step back from the old "hypodermic model" that posits that the press tells people what to think. For the purposes of this book, agenda-setting is considered to be the school attributing the greatest amount of real power to the press. Perhaps the most important point to be made about agenda-setters at this juncture is that most social scientists accept this theory as a proper description of the role of the press in the policymaking process.[2]

Of course, each of the three theories differs in how it assesses the policymaking power of the press. Those differences tend to lie along three separate dimensions: first, where the press gets its information; second, the tone and manner in which that information is presented; and finally, the overall impact on policy and the public.

As to the "where" question, the agenda-setting theory presumes that the press has varied and alternative sources of information. That is, the press does not rely solely on official statements or contacts for data on a particular issue. Alternative sources could include nongovernmental organizations (NGOs), statistical analyses and polls, and independent investigations.

Where the press gets its information is an important indicator of the level of its independence from strictly government-controlled sources. The independent press of the agenda-setting theory makes extensive use of non-government-controlled sources and data. This is not to say that, even in the agenda-setting approach to the media, some official sources will not be cited, particularly on issues pertaining to national security. In agenda-setting, however, the press balances both government sources and the official agenda with alternative, nongovernment sources so that it will have the capacity to pursue an independent agenda.

According to the agenda-setting theory, this broad base of information allows news organizations to emphasize an issue that is not necessarily a priority—or even a part of—the official agenda. Or, conversely, the media can deemphasize a priority of the government and perhaps even the public. Maxwell E. McCombs and Donald Shaw contend that the press plays a powerful role in setting the public's agenda. "Not only do they [the public] learn factual information about public affairs and what is happening in the world, they also learn how much importance to attach to an issue or topic from the emphasis placed on it by the mass media."[3]

From this perspective, the media are an independent variable in deciding what information to disseminate by giving the public cues as to which issues really matter. The press takes an active role in setting the political agenda and emphasizes specific issues or events that government officials (or even the public) would not necessarily select. By using alternative sources of information or by simply relying on its own priorities as to what is news, the press has the power to act independently of the government or the public in enumerating and providing context for its news agenda.

The manner in which the media present this information is another facet of the relationship between the press and the government. The agenda-setting school of thought contends that the press combines independent source material with a tone of presentation that is not just independent but often adversarial. Use of nongovernment sources allows the press to present alternative viewpoints on official policy. This leads to a greater capacity for critical review of both government policy and agenda.

Beyond source and manner of press content lies the final dimension—some say the most important dimension—of the media: impact. The agenda-setters believe the press has considerable impact. In his book *Channels of Power: The Impact of*

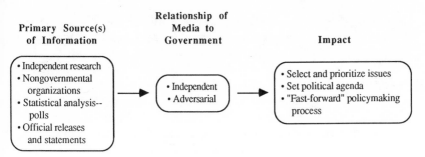

Fig. 2. Dimensions of the Agenda-Setting Theory

Television on American Politics, Austin Ranney argues that the media not only set the agenda but also create a "fast-forward" effect in politics. Ranney believes that the media have created a general assumption that "life's problems can be understood and resolved quickly, with no messy strings left dangling."[4]

Martin Linsky also notes the impact of fast-forwarding: "Policymakers understand that press coverage affects the speed of the decision-making process. A substantial percentage of those senior federal officials . . . cited the effect on the speed of the process as one of the most important impacts of the press."[5] These images put additional pressure on officials to act quickly, decisively, and, of course, correctly.

The media's ability to set the agenda—and to speed its pace— is the most widely accepted school of thought. Figure 2 illustrates a breakdown of the agenda-setting model according to media sources, relationship to the government, and impact on the official agenda. The agenda-setting theory has advocates from all sides of the ideological spectrum.

Lloyd Cutler on the left and Michael Ledeen on the right offer variants of this agenda-setting theory from their own ideological prisms.

In line with the general tenets, these authors acknowledge that media reporting, particularly television coverage, is independent and affects both the timing and substance of major foreign and national security policies. Thus the media do have a significant impact on policy in these areas. Cutler argues that television coverage not only tends to speed up the decision-making process (à la Ranney's fast-forwarding) but can actually set the priorities and even the range of acceptable options for the policymaking agenda.[6]

These ideas are not outside the general definition of agenda-setting. Both Cutler and Ledeen imply that the press is nearly omnipotent in its selection and presentation of a given issue or event.

According to this version of the agenda-setting theory, the media could almost be described as "agenda-dictating." Ledeen and Cutler are concerned with the classic notion that power corrupts and absolute power corrupts absolutely. They suggest that the ability of the press to influence, through selection or omission of issues, events, and even words and metaphors, should be considered among the most pernicious of recent changes in the U.S. foreign-policy-making process.

Most academics, however, refuse to take the leap from the agenda-setting theory to agenda-dictating. The majority of the literature falls into the more moderate category, considering the media to be powerful but far from omnipotent. Most agenda-setters do not adhere to the agenda-dictatorial notion that the press is able to exert dramatic or overwhelming influence over both the timing and the substance of foreign policy.

More often in the agenda-setting school of thought the press is characterized as taking an active role in outlining and prioritizing the political agenda. The press has the capacity to emphasize specific issues or events that are not necessarily part of the official agenda. By independently gathering information from nongovernment, as well as government, sources, the press is free to present that information as it sees fit and can determine the salience of relevant issues and events.

Agenda-Building

In *The Battle for Public Opinion*, Gladys Lang and Kurt Lang dispute this encompassing role of the media as the formulator of the political agenda and public concern. They studied the effect of the media, public opinion, and government elite on the Watergate affair and suggest that "the news media help to *build* . . . issues by establishing the necessary linkages between the polity and the public that facilitate the emergence of a problem as an issue."[7] Agenda-building, then, holds that the media set a process in motion by laying a foundation of knowledge for the public.

In the agenda-building theory, the government is the primary source of information for the press. Statistical data, independent research, and NGOs provide news and information that is independent of the official sources, but to a lesser extent than in the agenda-setting theory. Agenda-building thus is less concrete than agenda-setting. The press relies for the most part on official sources of information but incorporates a significant percentage of alternative material.

According to the agenda-building school of thought, the press is also less rigid in the tone it uses to present this information. The media appear less adversarial than in agenda-setting. Yet the press can use its access to nongovernment information to modify its presentation of official policy. The press uses these alternative sources to help interpret official policy, providing context, emphasis, and tone for government-defined issues.

The way the media present this information or create a specific framework for debate is another key component of agenda-building. How the media interact with information—providing context, emphasis, and vocabulary—is integral to its reception among the general public. Government officials are then forced to develop a framework to address the issue. Often this framework must take into account the original foundation (context, vocabulary, linkages) set out by the media. The type of information or the way the press presents it may foster preconceived notions about the issue in the public eye.

What most distinguishes the agenda-building model from the agenda-setting school is the conditional aspect of the press's impact on the public. According to Lang and Lang, agenda-building is the most accurate description of the impact of the press on the decision-making process. "The press itself [is] only one of several movers. Agenda-building—a more apt term than agenda-setting—is a collective process in which media, government, and the citizenry reciprocally influence one another."[8]

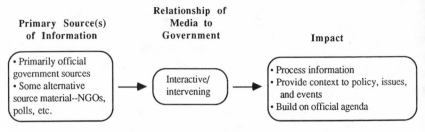

Fig. 3. Dimensions of the Agenda-Building Theory

Lang and Lang emphasize that the public may not accept the issues identified by the press as important enough to warrant its attention. So the press may present an agenda, but the audience may not be, and often is not, affected by it. Thus the role of the press is best described as an intervening variable; its impact is dependent on the degree to which the audience accepts or shares its agenda. Figure 3 presents a component breakdown of the agenda-building process.

In his book *Going Public: New Strategies of Presidential Leadership*, Sam Kernell finds a growing pattern among recent presidents of appealing directly to the public for support on policy. "The president seeks the aid of a third party—the public—to force other politicians to accept his preferences."[9] He notes, however, that in foreign affairs the president has a bit more latitude. "In the realm of foreign policy, the president may find a receptive audience among those citizens who would normally not number among his political allies."[10]

Yet, as an intervening variable in this process, the media play an important part in the agenda-building model. First, the media highlight a particular issue simply by reporting it. That issue is culled from a host of other choices, which, itself, implies uniqueness. The amount and type of coverage an issue or event receives will affect the range of its impact among the general public. More expansive coverage can result in a greater overall impact or it can simply produce a transient blip of public acknowledgment.

Agenda-building has a conditional effect on the public. Lang and Lang discuss at length the notion of the public's own agenda and whether the press reinforces this agenda. In other words, the critical condition is whether the public considers an issue a sufficiently important political priority and sees legitimate reasons for taking sides.[11] This process is part of a "cycle of mutual reinforcement that continues until politicians and public tire of an issue or another issue moves into the center of the political stage."[12] Thus the media *help* to establish the linkages between the polity and the public that can transform an issue into a national concern.

According to the agenda-building school of thought, the press plays less of a role in issue selection than it does in the agenda-setting model. The media, relying on a combination of government and nongovernment sources of information, act as an intervening variable. The press might provide the lens through which the public views issues and events, but it is the public, not the press, that influences policy and the political agenda.

Agenda-Reflecting

Proponents of agenda-building actually number a distant third to those who support an agenda-reflecting theory. Until now, however, this theory has lacked a name. I have chosen to call that theory "agenda-reflecting."[13] As the term implies, the theory suggests that the media merely reflect or relate the government's agenda, transmitting it to the public.

The question of where information originates focuses on the press's dependency on the government as a vital source of news. This condition undercuts the independence of the press, relegating it, in its most limited form, to something akin to an instrument of government. Some have even called the press the fourth branch of government. According to the agenda-reflecting theory, reporters' dependence on public officials for information undermines their independence to the point that they become simply transmitters of government views.

Lack of expertise and alternative sources puts the media at a disadvantage in gathering information. News organizations rely heavily on both official and unofficial government sources. For example, reporters routinely depend on press releases for the bulk of their coverage on government activities and policies. Leon Sigal points out that reporters' routine reliance on official channels allows the government to have a strong influence on the press's agenda. Thus he who controls the information controls the agenda.

The reporter cannot depend on legwork alone to satisfy his paper's insatiable demand for news. He looks to official channels to provide him with newsworthy material day after day. To the extent that he leans heavily on routine channels for news, he vests the timing of disclosure, and hence the surfacing of news stories, in those who control the channels. . . .
[Officials] are in a position to influence the content as well as the timing of news that reporters collect through routine channels.[14]

The independence of the press is undermined further by its reliance on unspecified (anonymous) government sources for news. Frequently, officials extend information to the media through "backgrounders," requiring that the reporter paraphrase what is said and attribute it to, for example, a "State Department official" or a "Pentagon representative." This process provides reporters with access to information they otherwise might not get, while giving government officials an opportunity to promote a particular policy or agenda without identifying themselves.

Particularly under the conditions of background, the media simply transmit this information to the public. This process of transmitting the news is an essential characteristic of tone in the agenda-reflecting theory. The press does not substantially interact or intervene to put its own spin on an issue. Information and expertise—even context—are provided by official sources. This dependent role facilitates the government's ability to manage the news. The media are little more than a conduit through which the government sets its agenda before the public.

In "Managing the Media," Philip Geylin agrees that "they [the media] are first and foremost a *transmitter;* that is to say the media do not create or originate the news."[15] Jay Rosen points out in *Democracy Overwhelmed: Press and Public in the Nuclear Age* that the reliance of the media on official sources not only is a reality but also makes some sense. After all, officials in the establishment have important "technical understanding or inside knowledge." But Rosen recognizes the potential consequences for a "reflecting" rather than a reflective press content.[16]

White House ABC News correspondent Sam Donaldson insists that there is nothing terribly wrong with this type of coverage. But Donaldson recognizes the consequences for what the news becomes.

I get used by the White House every time they trot out a story and I put it on the air in somewhat of the form that they want it on the air. . . . The President makes a speech and enunciates policy. He uses us, because he's communicating with the American people, but why not? We're here to cover his activities, and to cover his speeches, and if he enunciated a new policy, to put it on the air. So I don't feel that I'm being used in . . . some grimy sense.[17]

The "symbiosis" theory ties together where the press gets its information and how that information is presented. This theory asserts that the important thing about the press is that it is somewhat dependent on the official structure and its relationship with the government is, at most, interdependent. The press relies on the government, and the government relies on the press. If we were simply looking at press performance and behavior, this study might be able to stop with symbiosis. But this analysis is also concerned with and structured to include the impact of press behavior on policy. The symbiosis theory does not go far enough to take this impact into account.

As illustrated in Figure 4, the agenda-reflecting school is built on the basic premise that the press follows; it does not lead. In other words, the press neither creates nor builds the nation's agenda; it simply reacts to events and issues.

Unlike the role of the press in agenda-setting or agenda-building, in the agenda-reflecting model the press puts little or no independent spin on issues or events. Its dependency for information forces the media to act as a transmitter in conducting information from official sources to the public. Lack of expertise and alternative, nongovernment sources puts the media at a disadvantage vis-à-vis government officials. The press is

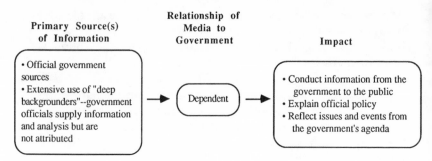

Fig. 4. Dimensions of the Agenda-Reflecting Theory

dependent on the government for material, and the government is able to set the agenda because it has a virtual monopoly over sources of information.

The Media and Foreign Policy

The three models—agenda-setting, agenda-building, and agenda-reflecting—not only generally are applicable but also relate specifically to foreign policy. The scholars who have written on the role of the media in foreign policy tend to be polarized and are primarily agenda-setters or agenda-reflectors in their thinking.

Of the dimensions used to discuss these theories—where the press gets its information, the manner in which that information is presented, and the impact of the press on both policy and the public—the question of press impact becomes the focus of the agenda-setting school. Lloyd Cutler's article "Foreign Policy on Deadline" echoes the agenda-setting argument that the press has a major impact on the policymaking process. According to Cutler, if an ominous foreign event takes place, the president must respond in a very short time. "If he [the president] does not have a response ready by the late afternoon deadline, the evening news may report that the president's advisers are divided, that the president cannot make up his mind, or that while the president hesitates, his political opponents know exactly what to do."[18]

This assertion refers back to the fast-forwarding effect of the press on policymaking. According to the agenda-setting school of thought, the media can pressure an administration to change existing policy or formulate policy on the basis of an alternate, press-driven agenda.

Agenda-reflectors, in contrast, look more to the news process than to its perceived impact. In a research brief titled "Foreign Policy and Press Performance," Lee Becker typifies the agenda-reflectors when he emphasizes the preeminence of official experts over the press, especially on foreign affairs. The question of where the press gets its information becomes the focal point of the argument. "Perhaps more than in any other area of news gathering, the press is dependent on governmental sources to provide focus for and information about world events. Since few newspapers have extensive foreign news staffs, most rely on Washington contacts for crucial information on international affairs."[19]

Other agenda-reflectors discussing the media's role in covering U.S. foreign and national security policy further suggest that the government has significant logistical and operational advantages over the media. First, the government retains a monopoly over the use of secret intelligence and other classified material. Thus the government has the power not only to classify what it does not want the public to know but also to declassify information that may advance or benefit official goals. Second, the government controls both the timing and circumstances of at least its own policy initiatives. This advantage allows a great deal of freedom in setting the policy agenda. Finally, the government can present facts and information selectively so as to place official positions and policies in the best possible light.[20]

It is evident that any consensus among scholars on the precise role of the media in the foreign policy process is elusive. As is true in the broader context of the relationship between the press and the government, academic and nonacademic sources support different schools of thought.

In fact, some participants in the debate between the agenda-setting versus agenda-building versus agenda-reflecting schools find it difficult to advocate one theory at the expense of another. Martin Linsky, in his book *Impact*, goes to some length to illustrate different (seemingly contradictory) positions on the role of the press. As he describes it, the media can be classified anywhere from "neutral transmitter" (agenda-reflecting) to "interpreter" (agenda-building) to "active participant" (agenda-setting).[21]

Rather than identifying his position on this continuum, however, Linsky covers all eventualities. "There was an overall sense that in general the press . . . was the dominant force in controlling the agenda." Later, however, Linsky suggests that "much of what becomes news is *transmitted* to the press by policy-makers themselves." Pinpointing the precise role and degree of impact the media have on official policy can be a challenging goal.

The press has more substantial and significant an impact on the process of policy-making than on the content of the policies themselves. Yet the press does have some very clear impacts on policy . . . there are some instances where it is clear that the press itself was the dominant factor in determining the policy itself.[22]

Resolution between the schools of thought appears no closer in the debate over the role of the media in general than in foreign policy making specifically.

The Press and Arms Control

What about arms control? Once again, the literature is sparse, and there are few, if any, middle-grounders who espouse an agenda-building theory of the press. The few pieces available on the impact of the press on the arms control process tend to fall into either the agenda-reflecting or the agenda-setting school of thought—somewhat surprising, given the ideological underpinnings to these two more extreme theories.

Michael Massing presents a clear case for the agenda-reflecting theory in his *Euromissiles and the Press.* Massing's piece, the only real attempt thus far to assess the actual coverage of the INF negotiations, argues that the *New York Times* "was so solicitous in its handling of official statements, whether Soviet or American, that it seldom tried to go beyond them."[23] Thus, according to Massing, the *Times* often relied on government sources of information and simply transmitted the official line.

Massing found that this type of coverage, from U.S. deployment of the intermediate-range nuclear missiles in Europe to the ensuing INF negotiations through 1985, was overwhelmingly slanted to a pro-American view. He suggests that "rather than serve as neutral observers of the competition between the Superpowers, the American media seemed to choose sides. And coverage of the Euromissiles suffered as a result."[24] Massing, however, supported these conclusions only with selective quotes taken from *Time* magazine, the *New York Times*, and the *Washington Post*. Massing's points are therefore based more on impressions and unsystematic references to selected articles than on a rigorous analysis of content.

In an interpretive essay on media coverage in arms control, Michael Krepon echoes the agenda-reflecting contention that press coverage of arms control either follows events or trivializes the process by treating negotiations as a "game." Krepon wrote that reporters treat arms control negotiations as a sporting contest. He argues that "media score-keeping" shortens the public's attention span to only the major events in the course of the negotiating "game." The story line is based on "winners" and "losers," "good guys" versus "bad guys."[25]

Coverage tends to focus on bureaucratic debates within the executive branch concerning the U.S. negotiating position. Based on these debates, the press then decides whether the United States "won" or "lost" the negotiations with the USSR. Subsequent Senate debate over ratification allows the media to cover both opponents and proponents of the treaty. After the Senate's final vote, the press analyzes the significance of the treaty in both political and geopolitical terms, assessing whether the United States was a winner or loser.

There are, of course, proponents of the other side of the theoretical spectrum—the agenda-setting side. In an ironic twist, the agenda-setting school of thought is perhaps best symbolized by Max Kampelman, who served as a chief negotiator on the INF accord. In his writing before becoming head of the U.S.

GROUP THEORY	MEDIA	PUBLIC	GOVERNMENT
AGENDA-SETTING Power of the Press: Independent	• Maintains alternative information sources independent of official bodies • Selects/emphasizes issue--sets agenda for debate • Informs/alerts the public • Raises consciousness	• Receives information from press • Demands government action • Sets tenor for that action in line with news agenda	• Fails to control agenda effectively • Reacts to public demand created by media-stimulated debate • Attempts to balance media on issue
AGENDA-BUILDING Power of the Press: Interactive	• Relies to an extent on official sources for information--not exclusively • Retains some input as to agenda • Controls presentation of information to the public • Shapes issue with presentation format--biases, individual worldviews, personal agendas, etc.	• Receives information from the media • "Attentive elite" fosters broader public debate	• Sets political agenda to large extent • Provides information to the media - attempts to shape media presentation of issue • Reacts to shifts in public temper • Attempts to modify public temper through media
AGENDA-REFLECTING Power of the Press: Dependent	• Depends almost exclusively on official sources for information • Adheres to officially set agenda of issues • Transmits/relays information to public	• Receives information from media as passed from official sources • Reacts to information • Confers positive or negative reaction to government on issue	• Acts as sole source of information to media • Controls news agenda • Succeeds in modifying/managing public opinion • Uses public relations to manipulate public opinion from bad news or press--limited

Fig. 5. Theories of Interaction: The Media, the Public, and the Government

arms control delegation in Geneva, Kampelman argued that the media tend to exert undue influence in foreign policy making. "The American press . . . [is] perhaps the second most powerful institution in the country next to the Presidency."[26] At that point, Kampelman was a strong advocate of the agenda-setting school. He warned against the media's abuse of their influence over public attitudes and their ability to shape the political agenda. "The media . . . constitute a powerful, ever-growing institution, with huge financial resources to supplement the power they wield through control over the dissemination of news, but with fewer and fewer restraints on that power."[27]

As a negotiator, however, Kampelman (perhaps without realizing it) was the quintessential user of the press in an agenda-*reflecting* capacity—both in his own thinking and in his behavior. In a personal interview, he acknowledged that he often used "deep background" restrictions in discussions with reporters. Kampelman went so far as to issue-specific ground rules, even putting the Geneva dateline off-limits for use in the story. The reporter had to use a Washington dateline to include material from the interview.[28]

Kampelman's ambivalence symbolizes nicely how hard it is to stay within one school of thought, let alone prove a school of thought. There is little doubt that the role of the press in arms control and foreign policy making is both confusing and conditional. It is important, therefore, to take a closer, more systematic look at the "wheres," "hows," and consequences of the press in foreign policy making. No single study can, beyond a shadow of doubt, corroborate any school of thought about the news media. This study tries, however, to find out which of these theories—agenda-setting, agenda-building, or agenda-reflecting—best explains the role of the press in both the INF negotiating process and, more generally, the overall category of foreign policy making.

Conclusion

The matrix in Figure 5 gives a detailed breakdown of the three theories discussed in this chapter. The theories are labeled according to the role played by the press in each. In agenda-setting, the press acts as an independent variable in its relationship to both the government and the public. Sources of information for the press in this case vary widely from official releases to material from nongovernmental organizations and independent research on the part of the reporter. In the agenda-setting theory, the media as an independent actor exercise complete discretion over the presentation and dissemination of information and even the selection of issues or topics.

In the agenda-building theory, the press represents more of an interactive variable. That is, while the media might rely more heavily on official sources of information than in the agenda-setting model, the biases, individual worldviews, and personal agendas of the press all serve to shape that information. Though perhaps not setting the agenda per se, the media interact with the information and the government to provide slant, context, or even bias. The government, in this case, has a much greater ability to set the political agenda and control the flow of information to the press but has only a minimal capability of influencing media presentation.

The agenda-reflecting theory contends that the government sets the political agenda and regulates the flow of information to the press: it even succeeds in shaping public opinion by and with the media. The press acts as a dependent variable, adhering to the officially set agenda of issues and relying almost exclusively on government sources for both information and context. Such a significant level of dependence relegates the media to the role of an informational conduit, channeling information from the government to the public.

The three theories, agenda-setting, agenda-building, and agenda-reflecting, provide a framework for analyzing the INF negotiations. The goal of this book is to clear up some of the confusion surrounding the role of the press in the arms control process. The book relies on both a content analysis of newspaper and television reports on INF and interviews with government officials and journalists. It is hoped that an analysis of these data will help specify the relationship between press, government, and public response.

CHAPTER 3

Network Coverage of INF

From 1981 through 1987, *ABC World News To-night*, *NBC Nightly News*, and *CBS Evening News* devoted more than 2,000 minutes of total air time to the INF issue. The sheer volume of coverage is eloquent testimony to the importance of INF in and to the media.

This chapter analyzes the network coverage of INF over those seven years. The broad question this content analysis seeks to answer is how the coverage relates to the theories discussed in Chapter 2. More specifically, can network reporting per se be clearly classified as agenda-setting regarding its sources and practices? Or do the agenda-building or reflecting schools better characterize the actual coverage? Various comparisons and combinations of data in the content analysis will help to define possible answers to these questions.

Methodology

Why Network News?

The major goal of this book is to assess the role of the press in arms control negotiations using INF as a case study. The network news provides depth to the study. It is widely accepted that the electronic press reaches a larger segment of the population than print news.[1] Most people use television news as a primary source of information about current events. Network news would, therefore, have to be included in any study of press impact, influence, or reach. Because this study is intended to be as comprehensive and inclusive as possible, using and incorporating data from this source was vital.

This analysis uses two of the three network evening news shows, ABC and CBS, as a basis for analysis.[2] News coverage from network to network, especially on a topic such as INF, did not vary significantly. The *CBS Evening News* and *ABC World News Tonight* were selected for two reasons. First, these network news programs have the highest ratings, which means they reach the highest percentage of viewers. Second, CBS has the reputation for being slightly more liberal and critical of the Reagan administration than the other two networks, while ABC is considered to be somewhat more moderate or at least less critical of the Reagan administration. Selecting these two presumably gave a more balanced ideological representation.

Parameters of the Data Search

When to begin and end. Using INF as a case study virtually predetermined the start and end for collecting data. President Reagan's speech introducing the double zero option on short- and medium-range nuclear weapons was delivered in November 1981. The data search begins in January 1981, providing a good lead-in time to discover any trends that might have occurred before the announcement of double zero.

The study ends December 31, 1987. The INF Treaty was signed on December 7, 1987, culminating that seven-year negotiating period. Although the congressional debate over ratification continued into 1988, the primary purpose of this study is to evaluate the impact of the press on the negotiating process. That process ended with the signing of the treaty, and data on press coverage of ratification were not germane to the overall goal.[3]

What to include. Having determined where to begin and end, the next decision in setting up the analysis was which stories to include. Key words, topics, and relevant personalities guided the search. All INF and INF-related issues were selected for consideration. The definition of a relevant item included all those stories that, in majority, deal with events, politics, people, or atmosphere surrounding INF.

The range of topics was designed to be broadly inclusive. Network coverage of European protests over the deployment of U.S. intermediate-range missiles was, for example, considered as important in the overall coverage as stories on the progress of negotiations in Geneva. Each of these issues represents a unique aspect of the coverage and, therefore, must be represented.

Dimensions of the Content Analysis

This content analysis focuses on strictly that—content. Excluded from the analysis are reporters' body language, voice inflections, and so on. The focus of the analysis was what was said, not how it was said. Others have criticized content analysis that ignores voice inflection or body language,[4] but it seemed unrealistic to make objective assessments of those very subjective things. Any indirect message the reporter seemed to be offering to the viewer was usually incorporated into the text of the story, not left to body language.

Also excluded were visuals. Although an argument can be made that visuals essentially *are* the content,[5] in this case visuals are practically impossible to analyze objectively in any but the most rudimentary ways.[6] Hence this content analysis looks at the text as the essence of content, if not the message.

Because of the volume of the data involved, the story itself is the basic unit of analysis. A story might contain information on different issues but was categorized as to overall theme or message.

For each story over the seven-year period 1981–87, thirteen different variables were adopted for the analysis. Several of the categories are standard elements: source, date, time (in seconds), and reporter. The remaining variables were developed to meet the specific needs of this study. These variables were used individually or in conjunction with one another to test each of the three major theories.

Testing the Theoretical Models

The content analysis for the network news will be presented in sequence. First, I test the content to determine whether it supports agenda-setting and in which ways it does so. Parallel studies of the content with respect to agenda-building and agenda-reflecting follow. Each of these sections will serve as a model. The models will illustrate how the respective theories can be applied to trends found in the data on network news from 1981 to 1987. The final portion will assess whether one theory is clearly better than the other two at defining the role of electronic media in the INF negotiations or whether the results indicate an ambiguous pattern of press behavior.

Before presenting the actual results, it is useful to define the specific variables used to test the data in each model. The variables will provide the basic criteria or framework for looking at the data in the following sections.

In the agenda-setting model, the press has many alternative sources of information other than the administration or government officials. Because the media are independent in gathering material, origination (or source of information) for the stories in the content analysis should emphasize variables other than U.S. government pronunciamento and unidentified U.S. government pronunciamento.[7]

According to this theory of relative press independence, one would expect to find more news based on multiple sources or investigative journalism. Such a finding would, in turn, suggest a greater propensity in the media for stories considered news analysis, as opposed to hard news. An analytical story, after all, demands greater input from the reporter's perspective and knowledge than does routine reportage.

Agenda-setting would also suggest that the press is most active in the period before the agreement process—driving events rather than being driven by them. The media help to define the issue for the public. The press is not following the government's agenda so much as promoting its own.

Working with the notion that the media have an independent agenda, the three categories critical of U.S. policy, critical of Soviet policy, and bias (or press preference) could indicate the direction of that agenda. If the press is pushing a specific agenda, media criticism of the United States or the Soviet Union will depend on which player represents a stumbling block to the preferred course of action on a particular issue at any given moment.

This same idea carries over into variables dealing with topics, especially with respect to their positive or negative themes, as measured against the government's agenda. The press puts pressure on the government to act on, change, or maintain a certain policy. Thus data or press coverage might indicate a particular bias by news topic. The individual topics in this category can be grouped to show whether the press was generally critical or supportive. Clearly, for example, stories about the growth of the freeze movement are negative regarding the Reagan administration's agenda.

Trends in the data that would support the agenda-building theory are not as well defined as those for agenda-setting. Although the press relies primarily on the government for information in agenda-building, it can also use alternative sources. But these deviations should be the exception, rather than the rule, if the agenda-building theory is valid. Origination in the agenda-building model should involve mainly U.S. government pronunciamento or unidentified U.S. government pronunciamento.

This model also indicates that the press tends to follow government-sponsored events. The media can emphasize certain aspects of an event or issue, though, that are not directly representative of (but are relevant to) the government's agenda.

Still, the difference between agenda-building data patterns and agenda-setting patterns in content is a matter of degree, not kind. In agenda-building, the press is dependent on the government as its main source of material but adds its own biases or, at minimum, provides its own context.

Trends pointing to the agenda-reflecting theory are easier to isolate. In agenda-reflection, the government provides almost all of the information used by the press. Thus origination would be grouped primarily in U.S. government pronunciamento and unidentified U.S. government pronunciamento. Consequently, agenda-reflecting stories tend to be straight reporting with relatively little analysis and heavily dependent on official quotations.

Because the government is the primary source of information in the agenda-reflecting model, the press coverage would, naturally, tend to be less critical of U.S. policy. This trend would appear in both the critical of U.S. and the positive and negative topics categories.

Overwhelmingly in the agenda-reflecting theory, the press is a dependent variable driven by the government's agenda. The media follow officially sponsored events and react to those events. The press does not precipitate or manipulate the administration's agenda but, instead, reflects it.

Which theory best fits the data? Let us consider that question using the same three-part categorization outlined in Chapter 2. First, *where* were the networks getting information on INF, and how does this diversity compare to the individual model? Second, *how* was that information communicated to the public, and can the tone of the story be categorized as either critical or supportive of administration policy? Only the third issue—with what impact—will be left to later chapters, which analyze personal interviews with journalists and government officials.

Agenda-Setting

The data presented here generally support the application of the agenda-setting model to network coverage. The number of news stories, sources of information for those stories, and even the type of news report all point, in large measure, toward agenda-setting. Levels and timing of critical and supportive network coverage also tend to give credence to the agenda-setting model.

Where the Networks Get Information

Agenda-setting presumes that the press has sources of information outside official government channels. Figure 6 illustrates the origination or sources of network news about INF, broken down into ten possibilities. Multiple-source stories were the most frequent throughout the seven-year period, except in 1981 and 1983.

The predominance of multiple-source coverage indicates a

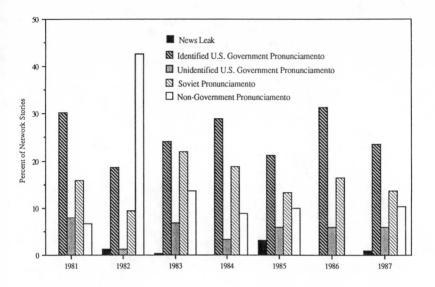

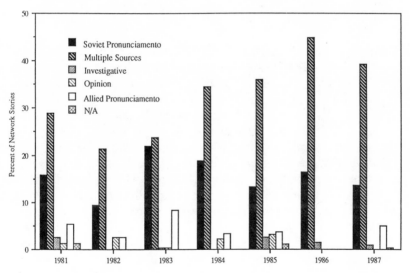

Fig. 6. Network Origination by Year

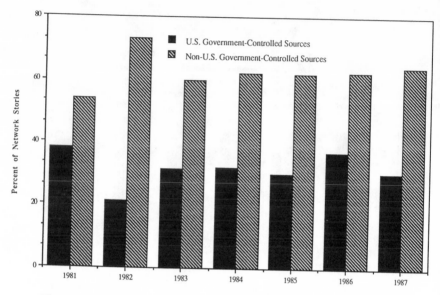

Fig. 7. Government- vs. Non-Government-Controlled Origination

strong agenda-setting trend in the origination of news. The networks were relying on and quoting a broad range of sources, not merely those of the government. This pattern can be seen even more clearly in Figure 7.[8] This graph shows that network news relied more on non-government-controlled sources in every year. The percentage difference between government and non-government remains remarkably consistent. Only 1982 is an exception, but it is an exception in *favor* of agenda-setting. In 1982, sources not affiliated with official channels were used more than three times as often as government-controlled sources.

These data show that the networks were using a broad range of alternative, non-government-controlled sources for information. This trend supports the agenda-setting model, describing the relationship of the press to the administration as more independent in nature.

Tone of INF Coverage

The second dimension in testing the agenda-setting model assesses the manner in which the networks presented this information to the public. Here, too, the data support the agenda-setting notion of the press as an independent variable in the INF equation.

The type of story used to present information serves as a clue about how deeply the media have probed a given issue (see Figure 8). Considering the types of stories that might be filed, the agenda-setting model suggests that the press would lean toward news analysis. News analyses generally use a number of different sources, not relying solely on official channels for information. In addition, an analysis implies a level of understanding and interpretation on the part of the reporter that would be found most often in an independent press. An independent press, again, is characteristic of the agenda-setting model. The data indicate that news analyses do represent a substantial degree—the second highest percentage of total articles—of INF copy throughout the period.

Now, let us consider news topics per se and determine whether the major topics suggest a news medium that was at odds with or compatible with the kinds of topics the govern-

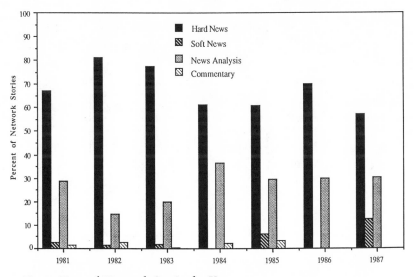

Fig. 8. Type of Network Stories by Year

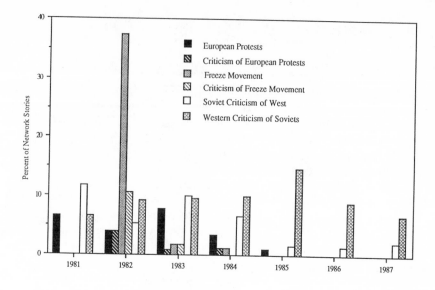

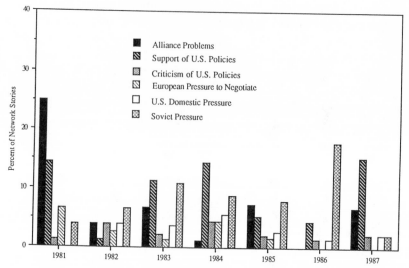

Fig. 9. Positive and Negative Themes in Network Coverage

ment would want addressed. Figure 9 contains evidence about the frequency of twelve major news topics. The data presented in this graph also suggest the agenda-setting model. In the early years, 1981 through 1983, alternative issues such as alliance problems, the nuclear freeze movement, and European protests all reached their highest percentages. In fact, these topics were the very core of network news coverage at the beginning of the INF negotiating process.

Of the twelve topics in Figure 9, eight can be considered as either positive or negative with respect to the administration's position on INF at the time. Four topics were too ambiguous to be regarded as inherently supportive or critical of the administration.[9] Stories covering European protests, the freeze movement, Soviet criticism of the West, and criticism of U.S. policies can be grouped together as being inherently "bad news" for administration policy or, at minimum, bad news topics. Positive topics, such as criticism of the European protests, criticism of the freeze movement, support of U.S. policies, and Western criticism of the Soviets, represent themes in network news that support official U.S. policy—"good news," so to speak.

Grouped together along these lines, Figure 10 shows, once again, that critical themes were most prevalent from 1981 through 1983. In 1982, news topics implying criticism of the administration received more than twice as much coverage as topics considered supportive. Perhaps more than anything else, these findings illustrate the independence of the press on INF during this period with the "bad news" focus overwhelming the "good news" focus in a ratio of approximately two to one.

The content data can also be used to argue that the networks generally favored arms control. Figure 11 suggests such an agenda. Although generally critical of the Soviets, the press was most critical of their policy in 1984. The Soviets walked out of the INF negotiations in late 1983 and refused to return to the negotiating table. Moscow's image in network news suffered as a result. The press covered "bad news" topics with respect to Soviet behavior as well, especially when the Soviets were not behaving in a peace-promoting fashion.

Criticism of the U.S. administration was at its highest from

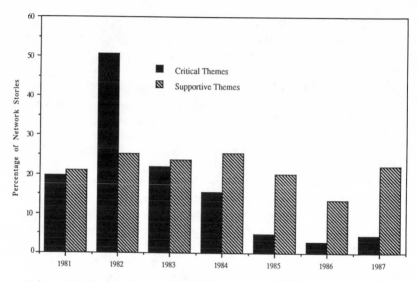

Fig. 10. Critical vs. Supportive Themes in Network Coverage

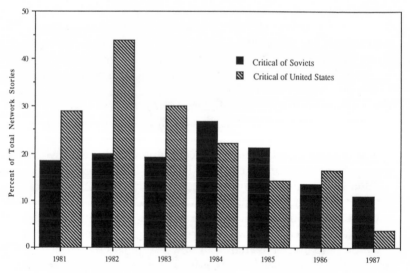

Fig. 11. Comparison of Network Stories Critical of the United States and the Soviet Union

1981 to 1983. Once again 1982 stands out as the year in which the press was clearly unhappy with the direction of U.S. policy. The turning point for the administration seems to have been that same Soviet walkout from the Geneva negotiations in late 1983. From this event through the signing of the treaty, the media seemed to be persuaded that the administration was negotiating and working toward an arms control agreement. Having been so persuaded, the press seemingly became less hostile in its coverage toward the more arms-control-committed administration.

Overall, network news criticism of government policy diminished once those policies began to reflect a more serious stance toward INF negotiations and an agreement. From 1981 through 1983, at the very least, the media were apparently doing their best to set the political agenda.

Looking at the data in terms of the two dimensions—where the information came from and how it was presented to the public—it appears that network news did indeed cover INF issues from a pro-arms-control position.[10] But what does this type of coverage mean for our pursuit of news theory?

There does seem to be a comfortable fit between news and news theory—agenda-setting theory. In fact, some of these findings go beyond agenda-setting, reaching to news bias.

First, during the critical early years of debate over INF, the networks focused on groups that supported arms control. This focus led to a greater variety of sources because the pro-arms-control movement was then at loggerheads with enunciated U.S. policy. Solely official sources would not have reflected this stance in these early years.

Similarly, when the networks perceived that the administration was inflexible in negotiating over INF, coverage of U.S. policy was more critical. The same pattern holds true for the Soviets. If the media sensed that the United States was trying to negotiate in good faith but the Soviets were causing problems, criticism of the USSR would rise.

When the United States finally closed the INF agreement in

1987, critical coverage by the networks of the administration's policy was at its lowest level for the entire seven-year period. ABC and CBS appeared to be pushing arms control and an arms control agenda. Indeed, once serious negotiations were set and an agreement reached, the networks backed off and let the arms control process follow its own course.

Agenda-Building

The agenda-building model injects an element of conditionality into the relationship between the media, government, and the public. The theory emphasizes the reciprocal, three-way nature of the interaction among these three actors. And network coverage, as monitored here, can also be seen as supportive of this notion that the relationship could be interactive—not independent.

Contrary to agenda-setting theory, agenda-building theory suggests that the media provide shape and contour to officially sponsored issues. This is an important, defining characteristic of the agenda-building model. To test for that form of press behavior—to learn whether network news was giving context, rather than a clear-cut agenda of its own—we must consider again the two main dimensions of content—source and manner—to decide whether the data support the agenda-building model of press theory.

Where the Networks Get Information

Looking at the origination of network news, it is clear that official U.S. government pronunciamento and unidentified U.S. government pronunciamento figure significantly in the overall coverage. But during the early period of INF the networks relied on alternative, nongovernment sources for information. At this point, as well, the media were covering the arms control movement with the greatest intensity. As part of the INF issue, this was still an aspect of the debate that reflected negatively on U.S. policy.

But the overall picture can be interpreted as ambiguous. The evidence on story origination (Figure 7) provides some evidence for agenda-building, as well as agenda-setting. Data concerning origination are at least partly supportive of the agenda-building model. Though agenda-setting emphasizes the media's use of alternative, nongovernment sources of information, agenda-building also allows for the use of both official and nongovernment origination. A significant percentage of network stories in each of the seven years was based on information from U.S. government-controlled sources. Figure 6 reveals that official sources provided material for the highest percentage of network stories in two out of the seven years used in the analysis, 1981 and 1983. In four of the remaining years, 1984 through 1987, the U.S. government was the second most frequently used source.

In light of this ambiguity, the question really becomes the way in which the networks were pursuing alternative sources. That is, did the press actually have an independent political agenda (agenda-setting) or were these sources sought out more to bring context and meaning to an existing political issue (agenda-building)?

Focusing strictly on data showing where the networks were getting information and what that tells us about the agenda-building model, it is possible to get an impression of how the amount of information from a particular source might affect coverage of INF. For example, in 1982, nongovernment sources were used in over 40 percent of network news coverage of INF. Figure 12 takes these sources for 1982 and illustrates what they were talking about. Nearly 70 percent of nongovernment sources were used in reports about the nuclear freeze movement. Over 90 percent of the network stories originating from nongovernment sources in 1982 favored a pro-arms-control policy.[11] Overall, then, more than 36 percent of network news originated from these pro-arms-control sources.[12]

This concentration of resources on arms control groups can be viewed as symbolic of the agenda-building model. The networks were able to highlight aspects of and build on the INF issue by using alternative, nongovernment sources of information.

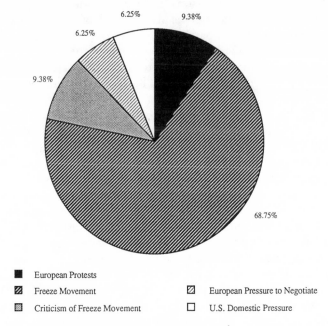

6.25%   9.38%

6.25%

9.38%

68.75%

■ European Protests
▨ Freeze Movement   ▨ European Pressure to Negotiate
▨ Criticism of Freeze Movement   □ U.S. Domestic Pressure

Fig. 12. Topics from Nongovernment Sources for 1982

Tone of INF Coverage

Data indicating how the networks presented this information to the public produce a similar problem: one interpretation
suggests agenda-setting behavior, another interpretation supports agenda-building. The ability of the press to take an existing issue and turn it into front-page news through saturation
coverage is characteristic of how the media build, rather than
create, an agenda.

What trends in the data might support the agenda-building
model by showing how the networks presented INF to the
public? There is some indication that the press was, indeed,
working to build up the INF agenda by establishing more recognizable links to other symbols on the political landscape. That
is, a double zero proposal might have little meaning to the
average citizen, whereas the peace movement or the idea of a

local nuclear free zone might bring the INF issue into a more familiar, recognizable context.

Figure 13 illustrates data on the focus of network coverage. In 1983 through 1987, the networks focused primarily on the INF negotiations. Naturally, in the first year, 1981, activity in the negotiating area would be limited. Because of the announcement of the administration's double zero proposal, policy issues rank high in the focus of network news. Geopolitical implications of INF were most often the focus in 1981, a likely result of the attention riveted to the administration's plan to deploy medium-range missiles in Western Europe.[13]

A dramatic increase in news focusing on the domestic political implications of INF occurred in 1982. Following the example used above, I isolated these stories, then determined what topics were covered during those news minutes. The nuclear freeze movement dominated the coverage, as illustrated in Figure 14. These data could indicate that the networks were working to build linkages and provide broader context for the INF issue. An across-the-board freeze on nuclear weapons not only is easier to

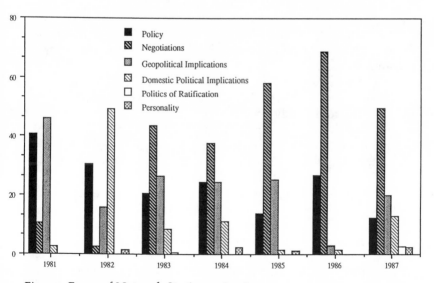

Fig. 13. Focus of Network Stories, 1981–87

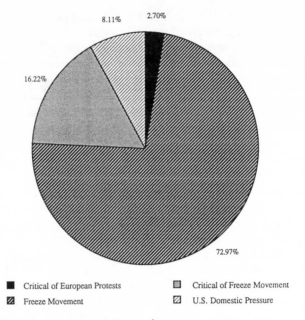

8.11%   2.70%

2.70%

16.22%

72.97%

■ Critical of European Protests   ▓ Critical of Freeze Movement
▧ Freeze Movement   ▨ U.S. Domestic Pressure

Fig. 14. Topics in Domestic Focus for 1982

understand than more complex reductions in specific classes
of weapons but also makes for much more dramatic news or
soundbites.

The nuclear freeze movement as a hot topic for the networks
in 1982 is best illustrated by Figure 9. A notable amount of attention—approximately 37 percent of network stories—was devoted to the movement at an early, formative phase of INF. No
doubt the U.S. government endured significant criticism as a result. How political figures view not only themselves but their
activities as reflected in the media is an important component of
the agenda-building process.[14] Fifty percent of network coverage
of INF in 1982 was critical of the administration (Figure 10). This
was the only year from 1981 through 1987 that critical themes
with respect to U.S. policy outstripped supportive themes.

Certain trends in the data on network coverage of INF can be
interpreted to support the agenda-building model of press be-

havior. Television news did not set the agenda for the administration—that had been done by the government itself, with the zero option. Nor did network news tell the public what to think about, for arms control was already an issue on the political agenda. Though the data are somewhat ambiguous, the evidence can be used to support the notion that network coverage tried to shape the INF process through context, issue directions or linkages, and focus.

Agenda-Reflecting

The term "agenda-reflecting" was developed specifically for this study and epitomizes the basic characteristic of the model. The entire premise of the agenda-reflecting theory is that the press merely reflects the political agenda set forth by the government when covering a given event or issue. According to agenda-reflecting, the media do not simply rely on official sources for information and expertise; they depend almost completely on those official sources.

This theory might hold true particularly in the case of arms control. First, serious negotiations are held in private, between representative government officials, which makes news gathering from alternative, nongovernment sources difficult. Second, technical issues regarding arms control—the weapon system(s), its use and function in military planning, and the like—require an expertise that is not often found among even the most seasoned reporters. So, if agenda-reflecting has utility as a theory, that should be evident in content data dealing with something as private and technical as INF.

What do the data tell us about the validity of the agenda-reflecting theory? Once again, as with agenda-setting and agenda-building, there is at least some supportive evidence for the model, and again, the issue becomes how much support compared with the other two theories.

In the seven-year period of INF, network news, in classic agenda-reflecting fashion, followed events; networks did not consistently get ahead of events. Although there are real deficiencies in applying the agenda-reflecting theory to the data, the evidence that does support agenda-reflecting is intriguing, especially viewed through the prism of events.

The Amount of Network Coverage

Media coverage of INF, or any issue, consists of peaks and valleys. Peaks in the amount of press that INF-related events received appear at the climax or actual moment in time that the event occurred. Because this was the case in five of seven years, media coverage could not have been the catalyst or precipitator of events during this time. The peaks in amount of press came ex post facto and thus cannot have been either cause or motivation.

Figure 15 clearly illustrates the event-driven nature of television news. Labels have been added to specific events that correlate with peaks in coverage. Rather than precipitating noteworthy points in five of the seven years of INF coverage, the networks reported on events only once they had become events. That is, viewed through the peaks and valleys shown in Figure 15, television news did not create the agenda for INF but reported on and reflected that agenda once the die had been cast by official channels.

Where the Networks Get Information

There is no question but that events drive news, and such a trend can be considered as evidence in support of the agenda-reflecting model. But what about other indicators? Consider, for example, where the networks were getting their information on INF. The origination of network news stories from 1981 through 1987 fluctuated to some extent, but as we have already seen, identified U.S. government pronunciamento consistently remained a significant source of material on INF.

Figure 6 illustrates the importance of government offices as a resource "well" of information. The data show that ABC and CBS drank frequently from this well, and in 1981 and 1983 identified government pronunciamento alone ranked first as a source in the origination of INF news coverage. Additionally, in all other years, except for the anomalous 1982,[15] official administration sources provided a high proportion (between 30 and 40 percent) of the information available to television journalists.

Alternative sources of information, however, made a significant contribution to network coverage of INF. This trend would be more in keeping with the agenda-setting and agenda-building models. Advocates of the agenda-reflecting theory would, however, insist that the press was simply covering events, not either setting or building on a specific agenda.

If the networks were simply covering events, then it would follow that the news generally focused on issues the administration wanted covered. Figure 16 confirms this suspicion. This figure is a variation on the focus of network coverage that links specific INF issue areas considered important to the administration with what the networks were covering. Both ABC and CBS focused primarily on areas that coincided with the official agenda.

From 1983 through 1987, the administration was concentrating on negotiations with the Soviet Union. Network coverage of INF in that period mirrored this focal point. In 1981, the United States was putting the plan in place to deploy medium-range missiles in Western Europe. Later in the year, President Reagan announced the zero option. Figure 16 shows that in 1981 network coverage reflected both of these selections from the official menu.

The networks diverged only in 1982, when the administration hoped to capture attention with the zero proposal. In this year, the highest percentage of stories covered domestic political implications of INF. Certainly, the political salience of the nuclear freeze movement as an issue in a congressional election year contributed to the popularity of the domestic implications of arms control. This trend seems to have prevailed despite the administration's best efforts to allay these concerns with the zero option. The next question would be how these events and this information were then reported to the public.

Tone of INF Coverage

We have seen that the electronic media received a large percentage of their information from official sources and generally covered issues that the administration had placed on the

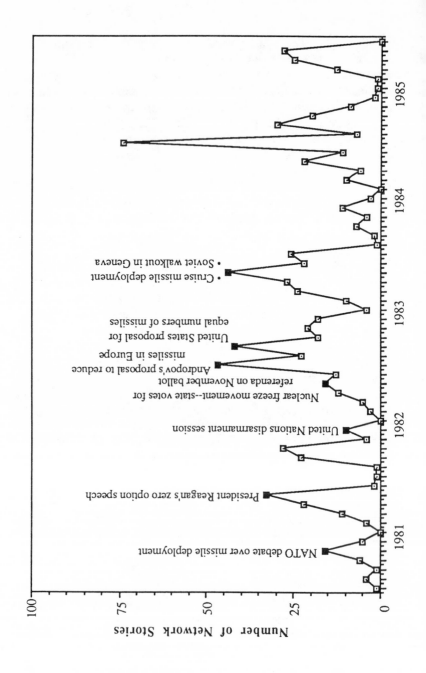

NATO debate over missile deployment

President Reagan's zero option speech

United Nations disarmament session

Nuclear freeze movement--state votes for
referenda on November ballot

Andropov's proposal to reduce
missiles in Europe

United States proposal for
equal numbers of missiles

Cruise missile deployment •

• Soviet walkout in Geneva

Number of Network Stories

100

75

50

25

0

1981

1982

1983

1984

1985

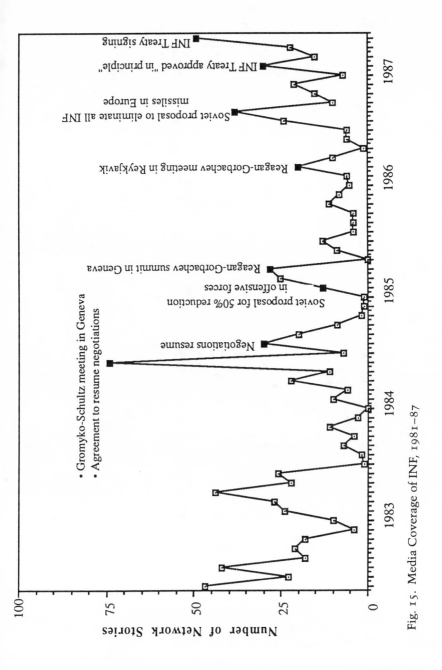

Fig. 15. Media Coverage of INF, 1981–87

Number of Network Stories

100   75   50   25   0

1983   1984   1985   1986   1987

• Gromyko-Schultz meeting in Geneva
• Agreement to resume negotiations

Negotiations resume

Reagan-Gorbachev summit in Geneva

Soviet proposal for 50% reduction in offensive forces

Reagan-Gorbachev meeting in Reykjavik

Soviet proposal to eliminate all INF missiles in Europe

INF Treaty approved "in principle"

INF Treaty signing

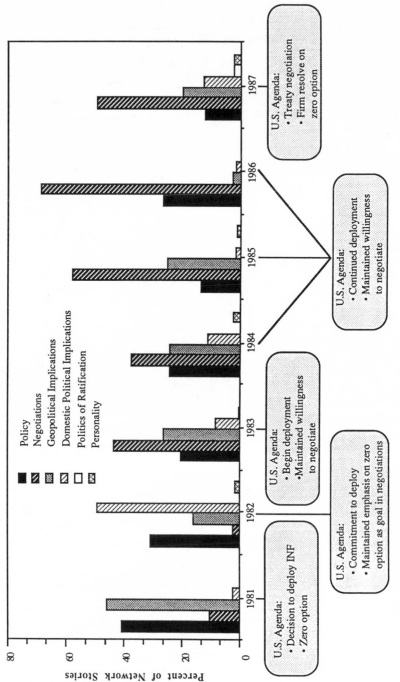

Fig. 16. Focus of Network Stories, 1981–87

agenda. But what were the network news doing with this information? How did the news reports treat issues taken from the official plate?

In the agenda-reflecting model, the press serve only to transmit information to the public. Interpretation and analysis are generally beyond the scope and role of the media in this theory. Thus data on how the networks presented INF can be very helpful in determining the utility of the agenda-reflecting model.

One way of telling how "reflecting" the networks were is to look at the data on critical versus supportive themes. Presumably, if the press was simply reflecting the government agenda on INF, reporting would tend to be inherently supportive of administration policy, rather than inherently critical.

Assessing these positive and negative theme categories in Figure 9 shows that for six of the seven years of the analysis, the highest percentage of stories reflected positively on government policy. Critical coverage surpassed supportive press only in 1982. This year was characterized by the predominance of the nuclear freeze movement as an issue for the network gristmill. In all other years, the electronic media, more often than not, presented a positive image of administration policy on INF.

Again we can see, however, how the data might be interpreted in contradictory ways. Though it is true that the network coverage was more supportive than critical of the government's handling of INF, it is important not to miss the shades of gray that qualify this interpretation. In the first three years, 1981 through 1983, negative press was a major factor in INF coverage. Certainly in 1982, when critical themes surpassed supportive ones, the networks were not simply reflecting the administration's agenda. In 1981 and 1983 as well, the levels of critical coverage were almost equal to those of supportive. The way the networks were presenting information on INF does not indicate that they were directly reflecting or transmitting the government line. In fact, they reflected the administration's agenda primarily when that agenda shifted somewhat in the direction of their own.

Event-driven coverage, substantial use of U.S. government pronunciamento, and a tendency to focus on the administration's agenda suggest that there is something to this agenda-reflecting theory of press behavior. It makes sense that on INF, or any arms control issue, reporters rarely have the opportunity to develop any expertise. Also, because the parties involved are governments, it follows that they will provide the lion's share of the information and that alternative, "insider" sources will be uncommon.

The findings, however, are anything but conclusive. The networks were *not* reflecting the administration's agenda in their coverage of the freeze movement or other themes that were inherently critical of government policy. This pattern is particularly true in the early years, the most important phases of development for INF policy.

Proponents of agenda-reflecting might explain this trend as an example of little more than "eventsism": the press was simply following events. But, on balance, there seem to be more data against the agenda-reflecting theory than in its favor.

Concluding Remarks

It is only natural to hope to find a definitive answer to any question. Once the research is complete, one wants to say, "this is *the* answer." The data on INF presented here, however, do not allow for one exclusive, "right" choice.

Clearly, a reasonable case, based on data, can be made for each school. It is easier to understand, in light of the content research outlined, the conflicting views about press performance and practice that exist in the literature.

Even when narrowing the field of study to arms control, it is difficult to assess the precise nature of media-government interaction—that is, news *process*. The data presented here go in several directions. Can the data—or the theories—be better sorted out and judged?

Figure 17 is an attempt to clarify the strengths and weaknesses of the three models. The chart shows the pros and cons of each theory using the various categories from the study. Breaking down the models this way makes it easier to visualize and determine each theory's relative merits. Often, it is as helpful to show how one model does not apply as it is to prove that another can be applied. It is hoped that this method will highlight the strengths in various arguments for agenda-setting, agenda-building, and agenda-reflecting.

To begin, the origination of network stories on INF over the period appears to fit the agenda-setting model best. In agenda-setting, the media use official releases and statements, independent research, nongovernmental organizations, and other sources of information. In using these alternative sources, the press acts independently to select and disperse news to the public.

Multiple sources provided the highest percentage of story origination in four of the seven years covered by INF. In addition, when the sources are grouped as government-controlled versus non-government-controlled, channels of information not controlled by the government predominate across the board. Figure 7, which divided origination into government-controlled versus non-government-controlled, clearly illustrated that the networks were not dependent on the administration as their sole source for material.

Government pronunciamento ranks as a significant percentage for source material, but the nature of arms control necessitates that the government be an important provider of information. Scheduling, progress reports, new proposals, and so on all originate from within the administration and must be included in news coverage. The data clearly indicate, though, that alternative, non-U.S. government sources figured prominently in the origination of network stories. The nightly news used official material but laced the presentation with additional, and substantial, unofficial information.

Findings that support the agenda-setting model logically weaken the case for agenda-reflecting. Alternative sources represent too significant a percentage of network origination for the agenda-reflecting model to apply in full. ABC and CBS news were not solely dependent on official channels for information, nor did they serve simply as a conduit for the administration's

	AGENDA-SETTING		AGENDA-BUILDING		AGENDA-REFLECTING	
	Strengths	Weaknesses	Strengths	Weaknesses	Strengths	Weaknesses
Origination	• Very high percentage of multiple sources throughout the years (highest in 4 of 7 years) • Overwhelming predominance of non-government-controlled sources in all years	• Identified U.S. government pronunciamento supplies a significant amount of information across all years	• Combination of government and non-gov. sources can indicate agenda building model • Networks didn't create 'new' agenda necessarily, but built on aspects of the official agenda	• Press was relying quite heavily on non-government sources • Difficult to determine if the network news was setting the arms freeze agenda, building freeze movement into an issue or merely reflecting events	• Identified U.S. government pronunciamento ranks high in percentage of total network coverage	• Multiple sources were also significant in network origination --4 out of the 7 years multiple sources had the highest percentage
Type Of Story	• Still a significant percentage of news analysis--not necessarily indicative	• News analysis not majority percentage in any year	• Type of network stories, though primarily hard news, was a combination with news analysis retaining a significant percentage	• Not all types of stories were represented in network news (limited commentary and editorial)	• Most of network news was straight reportage--hard news	• Soft news--presumably more characteristic of agenda-reflecting-- was only minimally significant in one year (1987)
Balance	• Good balance of source material with both U.S. and Soviet in the majority 5 of 7 years	• 1981 U.S. only was highest percentage • U.S. only significant percentage in all years	• Networks quoting a mix of sources throughout the period; relied significantly on only U.S. but also show high percentage of both U.S. and Soviet, and nongovernment (1982)	• Over most years, networks were relying on official U.S. and Soviet sources more than any others	• High percentage of U.S. only stories throughout the period-- majority in 1981	• Networks seem to use mix of sources-- both U.S. and Soviet tops out in 5 of 7 years • U.S. only dropped significantly in 1982

	AGENDA-SETTING		AGENDA-BUILDING		AGENDA-REFLECTING	
	Strengths	Weaknesses	Strengths	Weaknesses	Strengths	Weaknesses
Positive/Negative	• Networks appear to have been pushing a much stronger arms control agenda than the administration did in early years • Early years most important in agenda-setting--press took most active independent role (esp. 1982)	• Later half of the period, trend in coverage more reflective/supportive of official policy • In all but one year, supportive themes received highest percentage of coverage	• Network news was a mixed bag--although generally supportive, electronic media also pursued relevant issues that did not reflect favorably (i.e., freeze) on administration policy (1982)	• News stories were generally supportive of U.S. policies through period--limited evidence of networks building on official agenda	• Coverage was generally supportive of U.S. policy in 6 of the 7 years	• In 1982 the networks were highly critical of U.S. policy--this would not be the case in a strictly reflective scenario
Focus	• Networks tended to focus more on arms control in early years--more strongly than U.S. agenda	• Administration had espoused arms control agenda; networks not necessarily pushing in an area unrelated to official U.S. policy • Later years generally reflective of U.S. government activity	• Focus of network stories followed the official agenda but some issues covered relating to agenda were not necessarily those preferred by administration	• Focus simply reflecting U.S. agenda and events	• Focus generally reflective of U.S. official agenda	• Some areas covered (i.e., freeze) did not contribute positively to administration goals

Fig. 17. Breakdown of the Strengths and Weaknesses of the Three Models

message or agenda. In the end, the data simply do not support the agenda-reflecting notion of the media as a dependent purveyor of the government line.

The networks also appear to have been doing more with the INF issue than simply building on the official agenda. Dealing only with the origination aspect of network news stories, it is difficult completely to rule out the possibility of an agenda-building trend. Like agenda-setting, the agenda-building model assumes the media use a mix of information from official and alternative sources. The difference between the theories lies in the *balance* of origination. Agenda-building implies a heavier dependence on government-sponsored information. The network news data on INF do not show such a dependence. Indeed, ABC and CBS relied to a significant extent on nongovernment sources for material across the entire period.

The type of story covered by the networks also fails to provide certain evidence as to which theory best applies. Generally, agenda-setting would tend toward a higher percentage of news analysis. News analysis relies on investigative research and the reporter's own perspective concerning the issue. It is this independent contribution from the journalist that makes news analyses seem easily compatible with the agenda-setting theory. So there is some logic to believing that story type also fits more comfortably with the agenda-setting model.

Considering these strengths and weaknesses, which model "wins"? Agenda-setting seems to have the most support primarily because in six of the seven years (1982–87), U.S. statements were balanced with non-U.S. government, independent material. Such a persistent trend does indicate a news process geared toward agenda-setting. The qualifier here, however, must be that administration sources also figured significantly and, indeed, dominated in 1981. Although the agenda-reflecting model can be safely ruled out (in no way were the networks simply a conduit for the official perspective alone), the agenda-building model could conceivably be used in this case as well.

The focus of press coverage in the study lends additional credence to an agenda-building model of press behavior. But the networks' focus is only one part of the equation. We must also determine what the administration wanted the networks to report on at different points during the seven-year period. By comparing the course the U.S. government tried to navigate with the one actually followed by television news in the data, we can determine the model that best describes the similarities or divergences.

Some former Reagan administration officials attested that the zero option was invented to quiet widespread demands for greater commitment to arms control. These demands were largely created by the administration's decision to deploy intermediate-range nuclear weapons in Western Europe. It appears that the zero option was designed originally as a ruse to deflect criticism of this U.S. policy.[16]

Thus, from the government's perspective, the focus for press coverage in 1981 would be diverted away from the controversial deployment to the new zero option INF policy. In subsequent years, negotiations surrounding INF would, presumably, quell further animus directed at the administration's proposed deployment.

This plan met with marginal success. In 1982, the year following the zero proposal, most network stories focused on domestic support for the nuclear freeze movement. In isolation, then, this year represents a strong case for the agenda-building model: the networks did not create INF as an issue but certainly pursued an aspect that was detrimental to administration interests.

From 1983 to 1987, though, U.S. officials rested more comfortably because the negotiations were the overwhelming favorite focus in nightly news coverage on INF. This trend would appear to be more agenda-reflecting in nature (i.e., conveying policies from the official agenda). But one must also consider whether this coverage actually created a positive impression of the administration and its policies.

Evidence concerning how positive or negative the topics themselves were suggests some interesting conclusions regarding the tenor of the reporting. During the early years, 1981 through 1983, stories critical of administration policies were at their highest levels. In 1982, the coverage of INF issues was overwhelmingly critical of the United States. In the other two years, 1981 and 1983, the levels were much closer, with supportive percentages just slightly higher. These trends correspond to those found in Figure 11.

How do these patterns test out against the three models? First, the percentage of reporting in areas contrary to the official U.S. program and interests appears too high to represent an agenda-reflecting, dependent news service. There is a strong pattern of eventsism (of the press following events) in the data on network reporting. Peaks in the amount of coverage came at the time of various INF events. If the nightly news is event-driven in nature, it must report on issues after they are created, reflecting rather than nurturing the agenda.

Does eventsism necessarily indicate the agenda-reflecting model? Can the networks counter this through active selectivity? According to the data, the networks were apparently pressing for a strong move toward arms control—coverage of the nuclear freeze movement, European protests against INF, and problems within the alliance as a result of the deployment were at their highest levels in 1981 to 1983. According to the agenda-setting theory, it is this early period in the life of an issue that is the most important and in which the media can have a significant impact on policymaking. But were the networks actually trying to shape the agenda or were they simply building on the official agenda, creating their own context for INF?

This question is difficult to answer. The remainder of the INF period, 1984 to 1987, shows a significant drop in criticism of U.S. policies and a commensurate rise in support. It is also true that the seven-year period ended with a treaty based on the zero option proposed by the administration in 1981. These factors would point to agenda-building in television news—the media may have provided the lens through which INF was viewed, but the government provided the subject.

An agenda-setter, by contrast, would insist that the United States had no serious intention of following through with the zero option and that it was only through pressure from the media that such an agreement on INF was ever reached. Hence the networks were most critical of the administration in the early years to stimulate and solidify a firm commitment to arms control. Later in the period (1984–87), when the Soviets first walked out of the INF negotiations (November 1983) and then dragged their feet on an agreement, Moscow was likewise treated to significant criticism from the nightly news. The press can be seen as putting pressure on both sides to negotiate.

This point is important to emphasize. Although a pattern of eventsism is certainly present, we must evaluate the nature of the coverage following each event. For example, the United Nations session on disarmament in 1982 received a good deal of attention in the nightly news (see Figure 15). Network coverage peaked during this event, but the news did not reflect an issue from the official U.S. agenda. The coverage was devoted to an issue that the networks themselves included as part of the INF package.

Overall, the data could be "forced" to support any of the three theories by emphasizing or downplaying specific aspects. But, on balance, the weakest argument appears to be that for agenda-reflecting. The actual content of the reporting was more independent and less passive than this model presupposes.

It is more difficult to derive from these data on network coverage whether press behavior was, in the main, independent (agenda-building). A strong case based on the content evidence can be made for either model. But before deciding which of these two is more useful as news theory, let us consider one other type of news medium—what we now call the print media and what for so long was known simply as "the press."

CHAPTER 4

Newspaper Coverage of INF

All I know is what I read in the newspapers.
—Will Rogers

This chapter, the second half of the content analysis, continues to assess the relationship between the press and policymakers in arms control using print journalism as a medium. In the seven years of the study, more than 4,800 articles, columns, and editorials in the *New York Times* and *Washington Post* were devoted to various aspects of the INF. This number translates into 686 newspaper articles a year, 57 a month, and 1.9 a day. Nearly two articles, columns, or editorials were printed every day, on average, during the seven-year period.

Dealing with a data base this large puts even greater emphasis on the structure and organization of the content analysis. This chapter is similar in structure to the one preceding on network news. Every effort will be made to avoid redundancy but maintain clarity.

The first section is devoted to methodology, that is, the parameters for collecting the data, as well as how these parameters were established and why. Organization of the data is also critical. This chapter uses three overlapping sets of data from the *Times* and the *Post* to maximize the ability to discover and assess various patterns.

In the next section, the three theories or models applied in this study—agenda-setting, agenda-building, and agenda-reflecting—are used in drawing conclusions about the relationship between the press and the government and also as active "diagrams" in evaluating the data. I will discuss what one might expect to find in the data for each model, which will then help in determining the trends that actually exist. The third section will assess these trends using each of the models to interpret the data.

The final section will evaluate the strengths and weaknesses of each theory and discuss which one best explains the relationship between the press and the government in an arms control arena. In addition, I will draw conclusions from print and electronic media sources not only to see the similarities and differences between them but also to piece together an overall picture of how the press interacted with the administration on the INF issue.

Methodology

The *Times* and the *Post* were selected for several reasons. First, they are major news organizations with broad national appeal. Second, they are two newspapers of record, that is, they have established a high level of credibility for their reporting. Third, the *New York Times* and *Washington Post* devote significant expertise and space to international affairs, providing thorough coverage in areas germane to this study.

Most research indicates that policymakers consider print more important than broadcast news. The *Times* and the *Post* dominate the news chain in Washington.[1] These two print sources had the most extensive and sustained coverage of the issues surrounding the INF negotiations. Although print news does not have the broad public reach of the electronic media, the articles can provide greater detail and touch on subjects that might be more technical or not "sexy" enough for television. For all these reasons, the *Times* and *Post* were selected for this study.

As with the network news, data collection on INF-related issues in the written press began in January 1981 and continued through December 1987. Topics directly related to INF included intermediate-range missiles, deployment of intermediate-range forces, official U.S., Soviet, or allied statements or speeches on INF, the INF negotiations, and personalities involved in the negotiations. Indirectly related topics were broadly defined to encompass issues that may have had an impact on INF in some way. These issues included the nuclear freeze movement, European antinuclear protests, and the NATO alliance.

Organization of the data from the newspaper articles generally follows the same format as that of the network news. The first aspect of the print analysis looks simply at the amount of newspaper coverage across the period, broken down by month. This helps to establish trends in the relationship between the volume of news and specific events during the course of INF.

The second level of analysis parallels one aspect of the network analysis, focusing on positive and negative themes in *New York Times* articles.[2] Positive articles are those that support official U.S. policy regarding INF. Negative articles, conversely, are those that criticize the administration's policy. These data will help to show how the print press presented information to the public.

Because commentaries and editorials tend to be more critical of U.S. policy than news articles, such entries were separated from the main body of content information. In this way, data could be evaluated both with and without the highly subjective journalism one expects on the opinion and editorial pages.

Finally, a detailed content analysis was conducted of both *Times* and *Post* coverage, parallel to that used for network data in the preceding chapter. Only the positive versus negative category was omitted from this section because that aspect was covered by the second level of analysis on the *Times*. Because of the volume of data involved, a cross section of 10 percent of the 4,800 articles was selected in a random sample.[3]

Modeling Diagrams

What would data from the *Times* and *Post* show using an agenda-setting framework? One might expect the press to be more active in the early years (1981 to 1983). At this point, the press would play an active role in setting the issue agenda, fostering public support for specific ideas or policies. Also, print coverage might focus on related events sponsored by independent, nongovernment organizations.

Alternative sources of information (including independent research, nongovernment organizations, and statistical analysis) can also point to an agenda-setting model and be found in several categories of the content analysis. The origination of articles is one clear way to determine the level of independence on the part of the press with regard to source material. Identified U.S. government pronunciamento, unidentified U.S. government pronunciamento, and some news leaks are government-controlled channels for information. Nongovernment pronunciamento, multiple sources, and investigative variables would be highly indicative of independent information gathering by the press.

If the *Times* and *Post* tended to quote only U.S. sources, as opposed to both U.S. and Soviet or alternative channels, it would indicate greater dependence on the administration for information and undercut the agenda-setting model.

A high percentage of news analysis in type of article could also be indicative of agenda-setting. News analyses provide exactly that—analysis. An analysis, by definition, requires different sources of information and a certain amount of independent judgment or assessment on the part of the author.

The final dimension focuses on how the journalist then presents information to the public. The analysis of *New York Times* articles is based on an evaluation of positive versus negative themes or topics in reporting vis-à-vis U.S. policy. In agenda-setting, the coverage does not necessarily have to be consistently critical of the administration. That is, an independent press does not need to exhibit journalistic machismo by constantly criticizing official policy. What should be noticeable is a consistent pattern within the articles that both diverges from and coincides with the administration's line, depending on whether the press agenda, or "press bias," is being served. This pattern in the reporting will reveal whether the print press was interested in pursuing a specific, independent agenda and attempting to pressure the administration to follow suit.

Another element that might confirm or refute such a thesis is data from both the *Times* and *Post* on the focus of articles. Did the focus of the stories tend to follow government-sponsored events and issues, or did it periodically shift to alternative topics? Close correlation between the focus of *New York Times* and *Washington Post* articles and the official program would tend to undermine use of the agenda-setting model in depicting the role of the press in arms control. Divergence would increase the likelihood of an independent media agenda.

Trends in the data on INF that might indicate agenda-building are more difficult to identify with real precision. Though the press relies primarily on government-controlled sources of information in this model, it might also use some alternative sources. To the extent that the media in this case do rely on official channels for material, they can inject bias, worldview, commentary, and so on into its presentation. Thus the press creates a "looking glass" through which the public views information regarding (in this case) INF.

In agenda-building, origination or source of information for a significant percentage of the *Times* and the *Post* articles could be government-controlled sources. Balance within the articles might also indicate heavy reliance on official statements. The second aspect of the analysis (looking only at *New York Times* articles) allows us to see whether the coverage was generally supportive or critical of U.S. policy. Although journalists might use official channels for information, they can often play the "head against the tail." Conflicting views in different agencies of the administration (or branches of government) are not un-common, and reporters can use this material to put together a story that is critical of White House policy, even though the administration is the primary source. For the agenda-building model, it is important not only to see where information for the article originated but also to analyze the overall theme and tenor of the article.

Agenda-reflecting captures the notion of the press as simply a conduit through which information is passed from the govern-ment to the public. The administration in this model not only sets the political agenda but also retains a virtual monopoly on information.

This transmitting role characterizes the press as a dependent variable vis-à-vis the government. The lack of independent sources of information and expertise in the area of arms control forces the print media to stick primarily to straight reportage, rather than analysis.[4] News analysis percentages would be low because these articles would require both a broad base of information and understanding of the subject.

Data about the sources that would validate the agenda-reflecting model would reveal a high degree of government-controlled origination. If the administration has a tight hold on the information supply valve, it would follow that the material released would be generally supportive of U.S. policy. Thus we would expect the second tier of the analysis to show high percentages in the positive options—support for U.S. administration policies, western criticism of the Soviets, criticism of the nuclear freeze movement, and criticism of the European anti-nuclear movement.

The "head against the tail" analogy must be kept in mind here. The government consists of different departments or agencies, which are not necessarily in accord at all times on a certain issue. For example, powerful advocates or opponents of INF came to loggerheads, and frequently the *Times* and *Post* served as a forum for these debates, and, in the process, the reporters were liberated from government control.

One final point on potential findings within the agenda-reflecting model is the possibility for eventsism. The first part of the analysis traces the number of *Times* and *Post* articles by month over the seven-year period with certain INF milestones. Eventsism occurs when peaks in the amount of coverage correspond to a specific event. The extent to which this phenomenon might indicate agenda-reflecting depends on when these peaks appear and the activity that caused the surge. High points or blips in coverage that correspond to government-sponsored announcements or events would highlight that the official agenda was driving the news. Dramatic, sudden rises in the number of articles at the time of or after an event show that the press did not act as a catalyst for change or shifts in INF policy.

This trend would be the best indicator of agenda-reflecting; the media could not possibly be setting or building the INF agenda if articles focused on debate or related issues only once the ball was already rolling. In this way, eventsism can be considered the strongest evidence for the agenda-reflecting model.

Handling a large volume of data in the context of the three models has the potential for both confusion and omission. For this reason, each model—agenda-setting, agenda-building, and agenda-reflecting—is used individually as a framework for looking at the newspaper coverage of INF over the period. Each section is designed to present the best case possible and discuss trends in the data that strengthen the use of a given model. Once each case is made, the conclusion will assess the strengths and weaknesses of the arguments.

Agenda-Setting

Do the media behave in such a way as to set the agenda for U.S. foreign policy? Data collected from the *New York Times* and the *Washington Post* support the conclusion that the press did pursue an independent course of action. Many articles focused on related issues that confounded the administration's purposes, and the tone of the coverage was frequently critical of U.S. policy on INF.

If the print media were, indeed, acting as agenda-setters on the INF issue, what agenda were they trying to establish? Similar to the network news, the data point to a pro-arms-control tendency at work in print journalism.

Amount of Newspaper Coverage

One aspect of the agenda-setting model stresses the importance of coverage during the earliest phases or formulation of public policy. This is a critical period, during which public opinion about an issue coalesces and a political course of action is selected or shaped.

Figure 18 begins with a broad look at the volume of newspaper coverage over time correlated with selected INF-related events. The newspapers were very active in the first three years of the period, 1981 through 1983. The initial peak in print coverage focused on the debate within NATO over the deployment of American medium-range cruise missiles in Western Europe (May 1981). The final peak in that period occurred in November 1983, marking the start of deployment and the simultaneous Soviet walkout from INF negotiations in Geneva.

As discussed previously, press attention during the initial, formative phase of an issue may be evidence that supports the agenda-setting model. The level of early activity points to an agenda-setting tendency in both the *New York Times* and the *Washington Post*. The number of articles from 1981 through 1983 remained consistently higher than in the following four years: an increase in media activity occurred in 1987, but it was largely the result of coverage of the summit and the signing of the INF Treaty. Overall, the base number of newspaper articles from 1984 to 1987 was markedly lower than that from 1981 to 1983.

In addition, from 1981 through 1983, the press gave considerable coverage to events that were not government-sponsored or defined. During this period, the NATO debate in Europe over missile deployment, state referenda in the United States on the nuclear freeze, and a special UN session on disarmament all received substantial coverage, according to the data in Figure 18. None of these events were sponsored or authorized by the government.[5]

The findings appear to support the agenda-setting notion that press coverage precipitates government action or, at a minimum, precedes it. At the very least, the media, through their fairly consistent press coverage of the antinuclear movement, played a role in pressuring the government to react to those who opposed its policies.

Sources of Information

Data regarding the origination of articles also give more than a little credence to the agenda-setting quality of the newspaper coverage. Information from non-government-controlled sources implies a more independent press. By using these alternative sources, the print media not only can focus on aspects of INF other than those put forward by the administration but can actually promote an independent news agenda.

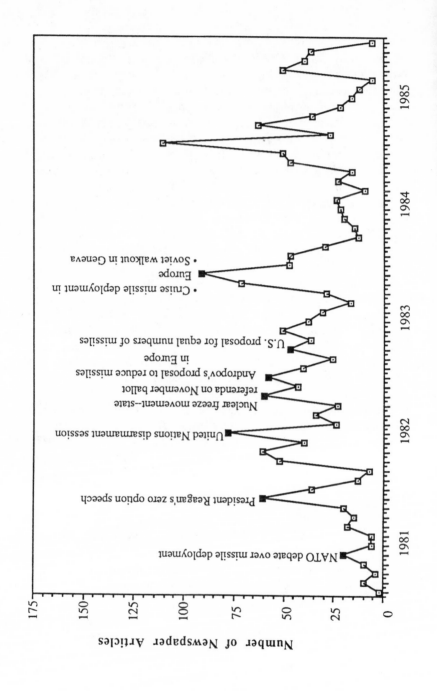

Number of Newspaper Articles

- NATO debate over missile deployment
- President Reagan's zero option speech
- United Nations disarmament session
- Nuclear freeze movement--state referenda on November ballot
- Andropov's proposal to reduce missiles in Europe
- U.S. proposal for equal numbers of missiles
- Cruise missile deployment in Europe
- Soviet walkout in Geneva

1981   1982   1983   1984   1985

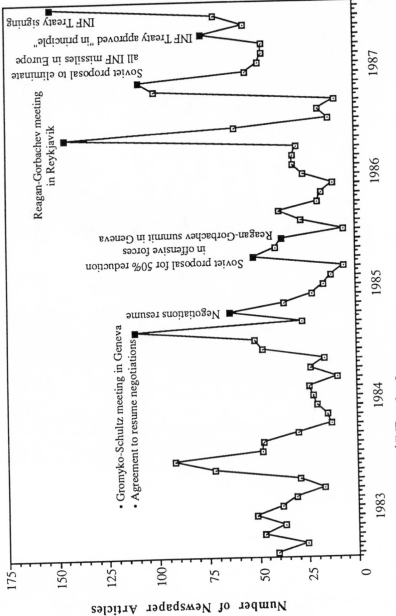

Fig. 18. Media Coverage of INF, 1981–87

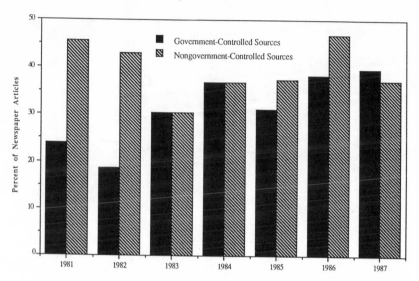

Fig. 19. Government- vs. Non-Government-Controlled Sources, 1981–87

Figure 19 illustrates that non-government-controlled sources held a majority percentage in four of seven years (1981, 1982, 1985, and 1986). Article origination based on government versus nongovernment sources was equal at 30 percent in 1983 and 37 percent in 1984. Only in 1987, the year the INF Treaty was signed, did the press use government-controlled sources in approximately 3 percent more articles than nongovernment.

These trends support the idea that in those critical early years of the INF period, the print press was building its reportage on alternative, non-government-controlled origination. The diminution of these differences in 1983 and 1984 suggests that the administration had shifted its policy or its tactics and that the press was now rewarding the government for its new approach in INF.

In the next two years, 1985 and 1986, the pattern reflects another form of agenda-setting journalism in which coverage became more positive once the press realized that government policy had moved in line with the media's agenda. Only in the final year, 1987, with the culmination of the arms control agreement, did official sources account for a majority of news origination (by roughly 3 percent). Information about an agreement, at this stage, did come from government offices. At this point, according to the agenda-setting model, the print media's agenda had been adopted—or at least placated.

Because of the international political nature of INF and arms control negotiations, official state organs are necessarily key sources of information. For the press to disregard them would be irresponsible. Balancing this information, however, with a combination of alternative sources testifies to a more independent press, one more given to agenda-setting.

Tone of Press Coverage

Let us now consider what this independently derived information was and consider, too, how it was presented to the public. *New York Times* articles were initially categorized according to subject and overall theme. A breakdown of the subjects is shown in Figure 20. This graph also shows how each subject stands in relation to the total number of articles devoted to INF in the *Times* during the 1981 to 1987 period.[6]

Looking only at the *Times* in the first two years, 1981 and 1982, one could make a strong case that the press's journalism was much in keeping with the agenda-setting theory.

A majority of articles in 1981 and 1982 covered the European protests and the nuclear freeze movement, respectively. Neither of these issue areas was controlled or driven by the U.S. government. The three leading categories in 1981 were generally critical of the Reagan administration's INF policy; these include European protests, criticism of U.S. policies, and Soviet criticism of the West.

The following year, 1982, the two most frequently reported topics were the nuclear freeze movement and U.S. domestic pressure to negotiate. Clearly, in these first two years, the *Times* was neither solely dependent on official government sources for subject matter nor was it driven in its reporting by officially sponsored events.

The year 1983 was the most active in the press for INF and also the most complex. For the sake of clarity, the topics of the

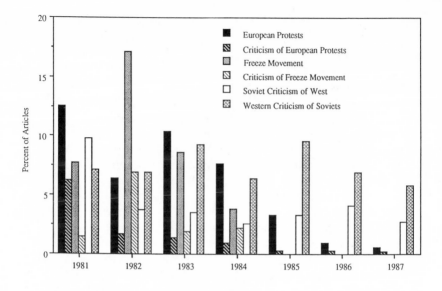

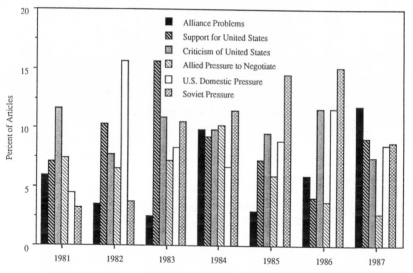

Fig. 20. Positive and Negative Topic Breakdown of *New York Times* Articles, 1981–87

Topics in Network Coverage, 1983

Topic	Percent
Supportive of U.S. policy	16
Critical of U.S. policy	11
Soviet pressure to negotiate	11
European protests	10
Nuclear freeze movement	9
Western criticism of Soviets	9
U.S. domestic pressure to negotiate	8
Allied pressure to negotiate	7
Other	5
Mechanics of negotiations	4
Alliance problems	3
Critical of freeze movement	2
Critical of European protests	1

stories are listed in the accompanying table in descending order of magnitude. These data might be interpreted in several ways. The *New York Times* had more articles that supported U.S. policy on INF than any other topic. The meaning changes, however, in conjunction with the remaining data. Eight of the nine subsequent topics (and three of the four highest) are either critical of the administration's INF policy or represent direct pressure on the United States to negotiate an arms agreement. Figure 21 shows that despite the high percentage of articles categorized as supporting the administration, overall *New York Times* articles for 1983 were more critical than supportive of U.S. INF policy.[7]

A significant percentage of the articles printed in this four-year period can be categorized as either critical of U.S. policy on INF or pressure for an agreement. It appears that what was being reported on INF by the press was independent of both official policy and interests at that time.

Even in 1987, when the INF Treaty was finally agreed to and signed, the most prevalent topic in the *New York Times* was problems within the NATO alliance. These problems were largely the result of fears among West European members about the agreement. Concerns over reduced security, potential de-coupling, and the like were featured in the print press even during the heyday of the INF Treaty.

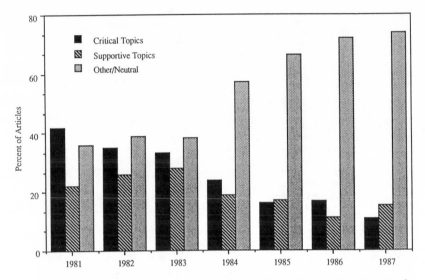

Fig. 21. Criticism vs. Support for U.S. INF Policy in the *New York Times*

Figure 21 provides a breakdown of themes critical of U.S. policy versus themes supportive of U.S. policy.[8] The graph clearly indicates that critical themes dominated the articles across the period with the exception of 1985 and 1987. Once again, debate in the press over administration policy was both most active and most critical in 1981 through 1983. The critical nature of the coverage strongly suggests an independent print press.

Though coverage was still predominantly critical, the differential between supportive and critical articles narrowed in 1984 and 1986 despite events such as the Soviet walkout in Geneva at the end of 1983 and the U.S. meeting with the Soviets at Reykjavik in 1986. Supportive press actually surpassed press of a critical nature in 1985 but only by the smallest of margins— 1 percent.

One would assume that the combined impact of the Soviet walkout and subsequent foot-dragging, as well as high-profile U.S. attempts to renew negotiations, might promote more support in the press for administration policies. This trend is not confirmed by the data, however, which show only a significant rise in the percentage of neutral articles (from 38 percent in 1983 to 57 percent in 1984). Overall, the data for 1984 through 1986 indicate that the *New York Times* continued to follow its own agenda and send out its own message with respect to INF, which was quite distinct from the official program.

The increased neutrality in the coverage parallels a more pronounced U.S. commitment to the negotiations on INF. This pattern corresponds to the idea that the press was trying to set an agenda (or, at minimum, cover an agenda) that favored arms control. When the government was making progress in this direction, the print media were less critical of official policy.

Two years that stand apart from the earlier critical tone of the coverage are 1985 and 1987: the *Times* seemingly shifted to support official INF policy. A slight rise in the number of articles supporting U.S. policy occurred in 1985. This shift can most likely be attributed to the resumption of INF negotiations in March and the first Reagan-Gorbachev summit in November of that year. Once again, positive movement in the direction of arms control is reflected by increased support in the press (albeit minuscule).

The rise in supportive coverage was more pronounced in 1987, the only clear instance when press coverage was decidedly supportive of the administration's policy. The positive response to government policy in the *New York Times* was apparently the result of the INF Treaty, signed in December of 1987. But this trend toward supportive press coverage actually reaffirms the notion that the press was pursuing a pro-arms-control agenda. That is, the only point when supportive coverage heavily outweighed critical coverage—in a ratio of approximately two to one—was in the year the agreement on INF was signed.

Content analysis of *New York Times* articles highlights some important issues. First, when analyzed by theme, or what the newspaper was saying, the majority of articles tended to be critical of U.S. policy. This fact is especially evident in the combined breakdown (Figure 20), which shows that critical themes predominated in five of the seven years. Further, percentages of critical coverage were highest in the early period, when it ap-

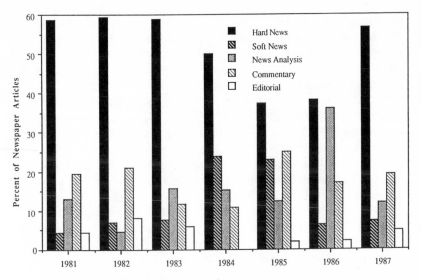

Fig. 22. Types of Newspaper Articles, 1981–87

pears the press perceived that the administration was not sufficiently energetic in pursuing an arms control agreement.

It might be argued that the print media (at least the *New York
Times*) were setting a news agenda devoted to an arms control
platform. In the early years, the topics covered suggested that
the *Times* was dunning the administration for not being sufficiently oriented toward arms control in its INF policies. By the
end of the negotiations, the news agenda might be viewed as
symbolizing a pat on the back for the Reagan policy. Overall,
however, the figures for the *New York Times* show that a surprising amount of what was being said in the media was critical
of the U.S. official agenda and policy on INF.

The third aspect of the analysis provides a detailed look at
approximately 10 percent of all *New York Times* and *Washington Post* articles. This representative sample allows for a
closer examination of how the print press was presenting information on INF.

The news approach in a given article can indicate a particular
model of press behavior and provide clues about the press-
government relationship as a whole. News analysis requires

both a high level of expertise on the part of the journalist and diversity in source material. Figure 22 shows that articles qualifying as news analyses represented more than 36 percent of the sample in 1986.

Figure 22 also illustrates the importance of commentary and editorial articles in the *Times* and *Post*. These two categories represent from 11 percent of the sample in 1984 to 29 percent in 1982. Figure 23 helps to illustrate how these articles affected the tone of the coverage. The graph shows the varying levels of support, criticism, and neutrality for U.S. policy on INF in *New York Times* editorials and commentaries over the period.

Figure 23 indicates that in every year, with the exception of 1987, *New York Times* editorials and commentaries were consistently critical of administration policy on INF.[9] Together with the volume of these articles across the period, editorials and commentaries were a powerful voice in the print media. These pieces called for a more flexible arms control agenda—an

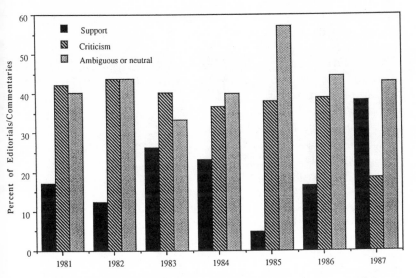

Fig. 23. Criticism vs. Support for U.S. INF Policy in *New York Times* Editorials and Commentaries, 1981–87

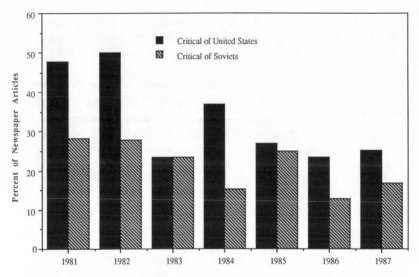

Fig. 24. Comparison of Articles Critical of the U.S. and Soviet Union, 1981–87

agenda not in line with official policy until the INF agreement was assured in 1987.

This criticism is clearly illustrated in Figure 24. Two independent categories of the detailed content analysis were combined to form the data represented in this graph. All articles in the sample were assessed to determine whether they were critical of the United States and, in addition, critical of the Soviet Union vis-à-vis INF policy.

This figure clearly shows that, without exception, articles from the sample across the period were not just more critical than supportive of the United States but were more critical of U.S. policies than of Soviet policies. Only in 1983 was criticism of both U.S. and Soviet policies equal at 24 percent. These data appear to support the agenda-setting model, pointing to an independent press at loggerheads with official administration policies. Some of this differential can be attributed to the language barrier and limitations on access to Soviet material. The overall trend, however, is consistent with an agenda-setting theory of press behavior—at least in these two very important news sources—the *Times* and the *Post*.

At each point in the analysis, the data could easily be used to support an agenda-setting model for the role of the print media in the INF case. The varying amount of coverage over the seven years from 1981 through 1987, as well as the content of that coverage, indicates that the *New York Times* and *Washington Post* were pursuing an independent agenda, and a pro-arms-control agenda at that.

The first portion of the analysis, detailing the actual number of articles with specific INF-related events year by year, showed that the print press was most active in the early years, 1981 through 1983. These three years were critical in the formative process of INF as an issue. This time frame is important in reference to agenda-setting because it is the point at which new information can be introduced and public opinion is shaped.

Also important in the agenda-setting model is how the media fulfill the task of educating and informing the public. If the press is dependent solely on the government not only for information but for a program of events, then the media are simply following, not leading, let alone setting, an agenda. These data from the *New York Times* and *Washington Post* during the initial phase, 1981–83, indicate that the newspapers were taking something approaching a lead in independently pursuing INF-related issues. Events not sponsored by the U.S. government, including the UN session on disarmament and the campaign for state referenda on the nuclear freeze, commanded high levels of coverage and imply that the *Times* and the *Post* were, at minimum, trying to set the INF agenda.

Where the print media were getting information also supports an agenda-setting model. In the first six years of the period, 1981 through 1986, both newspapers based INF coverage predominantly on non-government-controlled sources. These alternative avenues of information are a crucial component of the agenda-setting theory. They allow the press to act independently to disperse and interpret news and issues.

Findings that focused specifically on the *New York Times* were consistent with this general conclusion. Once again, early in the period, 1981 through 1983, articles focused primarily on topics critical of U.S. policy on INF. European protests against the deployment of medium-range weapons in Western Europe and the movement advocating a nuclear freeze figured prominently in these years. This coverage was neither dependent on the government as a source of information nor driven by official events or leads.

Setting a pro-arms-control agenda in the coverage was also suggested by the significant number of articles (1981 through 1986) that were critical of U.S. policy. Indeed, the coverage remained critical until 1987. Only in that year did the *Times* devote more of its news to supportive than to critical coverage.

The third section of the analysis provided a more detailed look at the content of the coverage from both the *Times* and the *Post* and allowed some of each story to be identified and coded. News analysis made up a significant percentage of the coverage across all seven years, implying an agenda-setting pattern of news reporting.

The basic message appears to be that both the *New York Times* and the *Washington Post*, at minimum, attempted to set an agenda by the news they selected and presented. The data in this section could easily be used to support the notion that the print media—at least the elite print media—were trying to play an active, agenda-setting role—not just following official policy on arms control and the INF issue. But can a similar analysis of the content find evidence to support the second, less aggressive, model of press and policy, the agenda-building model?

Agenda-Building

In agenda-building, the press does not take an active part in the selection of issues, but rather interprets and presents official policies and events. The method of issue presentation, including specific vocabulary, additional commentary, and information sources, can be a critical factor in how that issue or event is perceived by the public.

This intervening function of the media and its subsequent impact on public opinion are key aspects of agenda-building. The data gathered from the *New York Times* and *Washington Post* provide some clues about how the press was, on occasion, an interactive agent, not a dominating force, in processing information regarding INF between the government and the public.

Content data collected from both the *Times* and the *Post* can be used to support an agenda-building model for the press. Consider this example: President Reagan's proposal of the zero option in November 1981 was the first milestone in the INF study period. Content evidence from these two newspapers suggests that the print media seized on the idea of arms control and an agreement on INF. It must be remembered, however, that the government took the initiative—it introduced the zero option. The press then grabbed hold of the government's idea.

The levels of coverage critical or supportive of administration policy on INF varied, depending on the degree to which the press was seemingly building on aspects of the INF issue. It is important, however, to note in the data that follow that neither the *New York Times* nor the *Washington Post* created *new* issues or *new* options, but they made much out of those the government had presented that they liked and, conversely, made little of those for which they did not care.

In this process, the media relied on information from a combination of both government and non-government-controlled sources—again, a sign that supports an agenda-building theory of press behavior. According to the analysis that closely examines a representative cross section of *New York Times* and *Washington Post* articles, official channels provided many, but not all, of the sources used to build the news. Nongovernment organizations, polling data, and other sources helped round out the articles and provide context to issues from the official slate.

It is this sense of the press interacting with a given issue, exploring various tangents and providing a unique context, that symbolizes the agenda-building model. Press coverage in this instance need not—and did not—always reflect positively on official policy. But by building on the government's agenda, the press was capable of being an active, that is, interactive, element in presenting options to other leaders and the public. The print media, though not necessarily *setting* the political agenda, had an ability and a tendency to interact with the government and to present options.

Overall, the press, according to the agenda-building model, does just that—it builds on the official agenda. The data below suggest that there is evidence to support agenda-building, in the way the elite press discovered, analyzed, and presented the news.

Level of Newspaper Coverage

The number of articles appearing in the *New York Times* and *Washington Post* between 1981 and 1987 (Figure 18), indicate that the peaks in coverage correspond to specific events across the period. The first significant surge in coverage occurred in May 1981, when the Reagan administration lobbied the Western European members of NATO to accept deployment of American medium-range nuclear weapons in the theater. Only six months later, in November 1981, President Reagan presented his double zero arms proposal.

The events that produced these peaks in the *Times* and *Post* coverage can easily be regarded as a mix of government and non-government-sponsored initiatives. The timing and nature of the events could, indeed, support an agenda-building model. The non-government-sponsored events were concentrated in the early phase of the INF period. Both the United Nations disarmament session and the movement for individual state referenda supporting a nuclear freeze took place in 1982. According to the agenda-building model of press behavior, in this initial phase the media put together context and provide saturation coverage of individual issues that is then passed along to the public.

After President Reagan's announcement of double zero in November 1981, the *Times* and *Post* focused on arms control movements not engineered or controlled by the official government. Although the administration had developed an INF-related platform issue (double zero), the media chose to investigate the relationship between INF and arms control from an alternate perspective.

This pattern typifies the agenda-building model, in which the press is an interactive variable in presenting information on official policy to the public. The U.S. government laid the foundation of its agenda in the form of the double zero option; the print media reported on this proposal. But thereafter, the press built on the INF–arms control issue using nongovernment means and methods. Though subsequent reporting addressed arms control—an issue already on the official agenda—coverage was characterized by a nonofficial viewpoint.[10]

An important part of the press's role in agenda-building is to interpret various issues and events for the public. Hence at times, issues the administration might prefer to ignore will be reported—and might even become focal points for debate. It appears that the INF agenda had been set by the government's zero option. Thus the print media did not put arms control per se on the agenda. Yet by focusing on areas such as the domestic movement for a nuclear freeze and the UN disarmament session, the *New York Times* and *Washington Post* seem to have put a particular spin on the INF issue. "Spin" is defined here not so much as the news that is pro or con on the policy question but as the kinds of stories the press chooses to mix in with the hard news. The administration might have controlled the agenda, but the press built on that agenda with context, commentary, and worldview.

Sources of Information

Based on the origination (or source) of news, one might readily accept the thesis that the press builds more than it sets the agenda.[11] Data concerning the sources of news could be used to argue that the print press was interacting with, but not determining, the policy agenda.

Figure 25 shows that origination of press coverage during the period was a mix of both government and nongovernment sources. Identified U.S. government pronunciamento was a significant avenue of information throughout the seven years of

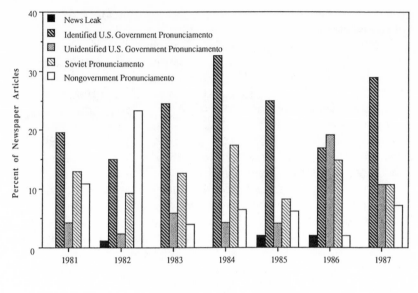

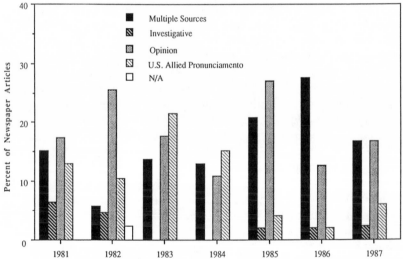

Fig. 25. Origination of Newspaper Articles, 1981–87

the study, from a low of 15 percent in 1982 to a high of 33 percent in 1984. Origination from strictly nongovernment pronunciamento reached a peak in 1982 of 23 percent but dropped off in subsequent years.

Clearly, the print media relied on a combination of sources as the basis for articles dealing with INF. The data seem, in this light, to complement the agenda-building notion of a balance of sources. Although the government did provide a significant amount of information, particularly on an arms control–national security issue, alternative nonofficial material also figured prominently in the coverage.

Figure 19 illustrates the trends in government-controlled versus non-government-controlled origination for *Times* and *Post* coverage of INF. Percentages from 1981 and 1982 indicate that the press was building on the administration's agenda, using significantly larger amounts of information over which the government had no control (22 percent higher in 1981 and 24 percent higher in 1982).

This combination of official and alternative sources is a fundamental characteristic of the agenda-building model. In the last five years of the period, from 1983 through 1987, the difference between government-controlled and non-government-controlled sources was never higher than 8.5 percent. In this sense, the press did appear to be building on the official agenda early in the study, using a higher percentage of alternative origination. In later years, once the context and spin were in place, the print media relied in near equal measure on government and nongovernment source material.

The balance of sources cited in the *Times* and *Post* articles on INF indicates a similar mix in the sourcing of news. Figure 26 shows that official U.S. sources were quoted most frequently throughout the period. Only in 1983 did more articles cite U.S. allies by 3 percent over U.S.-only sources. Generally, however, although U.S. sources were consistently used more often, other sources made a significant contribution to the total news package.

In determining where the press got information on INF, the data show a mix of government-controlled and non-govern-

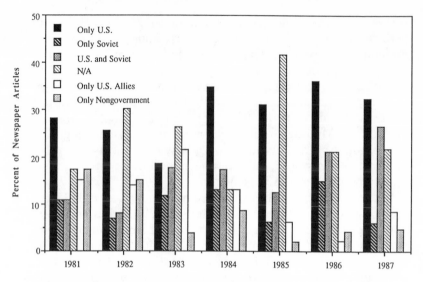

Fig. 26. Balance in Newspaper Articles, 1981–87

ment-controlled sources in both origination and balance of *New York Times* and *Washington Post* articles. This trend corresponds nicely with the tenets of the agenda-building model. The 10 percent sample indicates that the press relied on both the administration and alternative sources.

This balance between sources and the use of non-government-controlled information could imply a press that builds on the government's initial agenda. In fact, the media did not create the deployment of, negotiations about, or agreement on intermediate-range nuclear forces as issues for public consumption. All the components of INF were part of the official agenda. The print media, however, did appear to have used alternative sources to create context and unique insights into the government's INF program.

Tone of INF Coverage

In the agenda-building model, the media play an important role in "packaging" issues for public consumption. This packaging or presentation can have an important effect on both public opinion and official policy. The second aspect of the analysis focuses on *New York Times* articles across the seven-year period, categorizing these articles by overall topic. In this way, the frequency of specific topics is assessed and general patterns in the coverage and how those patterns relate to government policy emerge.

By grouping certain topics together, it is possible to determine whether the reporting reflected positively or negatively on the administration's handling of the INF issue. Figure 21 illustrates the changes in the levels of criticism, support, and neutrality over time. In the last four years of the study, 1984 through 1987, there were minimal differentials between criticism and support for official policy (from 1 percent in 1985 to 6 percent in 1986). The most dramatic trend during these four years was the marked increase in the number of neutral articles (from 57 percent in 1984 up to 74 percent in 1987).

The higher percentage of neutral coverage from 1984 through 1987 should be viewed in the context of what came before. Figure 21 indicates that from 1981 through 1983, the press was building on the INF agenda. The double zero proposal had been introduced by the Reagan administration, making arms control part of the official INF agenda. The media actively pursued this idea of an agreement on medium-range missiles and the general principle of nuclear disarmament.

In focusing on this aspect, *New York Times* coverage of U.S. policy in the first three years was decidedly negative. The news media were building a frame of reference for the public that emphasized arms control. The government, conversely, from 1981 through 1983, was firmly committed to the deployment of intermediate-range nuclear forces in Western Europe. The combination of these two factors created a swell of criticism against U.S. policy in the press during the early three-year period.[12]

Taken together with the increased neutrality of *New York Times* coverage from 1984 through 1987, these trends could well be viewed as supportive of the agenda-building model. That is, the press was building on the agenda in the first three years, reporting heavily on arms control aspects of INF. The government, at that time, was not focusing on arms control but on deployment. This combination resulted in higher levels of coverage that reflected negatively on U.S. policy. In the latter half of the period (1984 to 1987), once the administration turned seriously to arms control, the amount of critical coverage dropped and the number of neutral articles rose substantially. This pattern would appear to indicate that saturation coverage of issues such as the nuclear freeze movement, evident in the early years, had given way to more objective or neutral reporting.

Content data from the *New York Times* and *Washington Post* can be interpreted as supportive of an agenda-building model of press practice and performance. The print media took an active role in presenting and interpreting events and relevant U.S. policies. In this way, the press constructed a framework for INF, using a worldview and creating a spin independent of the administration and its platform. Though agenda-building hinges on the conditionality of the amount of impact the media eventually had on public opinion, there is, at this point, little doubt that agenda-building theorists such as Kurt and Gladys Lang could use these content data to reinforce their theory of press-elite interaction, as opposed to media dictation of news and the agenda.

Overall, the data show that both the *Times* and the *Post* devoted a significant amount of coverage to the INF issue. Peaks in the number of articles are primarily keyed to officially sponsored events. This is not the case, however, in 1982. The two surges in coverage for this year correlate to INF-related events that were not sponsored by the U.S. government. These events, the UN session on disarmament and the call for state referenda supporting a nuclear freeze, were dedicated to the arms control aspect of INF. The press was building on this arms limitation aspect of the official agenda at a time when the administration itself was lobbying hard for deployment of INF.

An important part of the agenda-building model contends that the media investigate and expand on aspects of a given issue. Certain areas that the press sensed had been ignored or misrepresented by the government would be targeted for saturated, independently researched reporting. The print media do not select or formulate the agenda but look for previously ne-

glected or unexplored angles. The press then serves as an intervening variable in presenting issues from the official agenda
with its own twist to the public.

Origination in INF coverage showed a similar building pattern in the first years of the period. The *Times* and *Post* were
tapping into alternative sources of information, particularly in
1981 and 1982. At that time the press was focusing on an aspect
of INF (arms control) to which the government was not particularly attentive. Thus in investigating and reporting on arms
control, the media turned to alternative, non-government-
controlled sources for material.

It is important to note, however, that U.S. government pronunciamento served as a major source of news throughout the
period. But this reality is not wholly inconsistent with the
tenets of agenda-building. Agenda-building suggests a press that
uses a compendium of both official and unofficial channels for
information. Indeed, many aspects of INF are legitimately considered part of the nation's security. Hence inclusion and participation of government sources is not only appropriate but
essential in any model of press behavior.

The agenda-building model suggests a rather specific relationship between the government and the press. In this model,
the media interact with the official agenda. The press, rather
than actually setting the political agenda, builds on issues set
forth by the administration and provides a framework for those
issues within the popular domain. The data indicate that the
Times and *Post* at times provided a context for INF that was
both a mixture of sources and interactive in nature—reporting
in an agenda-building style and tone.

Agenda-Reflecting

An agenda-reflecting press neither sets nor builds the agenda;
it "mouths" the agenda set forth by political elites. In the
agenda-reflecting model, the media represent a dependent variable, relying almost solely on official sources for information.
INF specifically and arms control generally are particularly
likely to produce evidence for this model. Because negotiations

are conducted between governments and often held in private sessions, government officials hold a virtual monopoly over relevant information. In addition, these officials frequently develop a level of expertise greater than that of the journalists, who are routinely shifted from one assignment to the next.

Data collected from the *New York Times* and *Washington Post* over the seven-year study of INF could be interpreted to mean that coverage did reflect the administration's program. The most telling example is the fact that President Reagan proposed the zero option for INF in 1981 and the INF Treaty signed by the United States and Soviet Union in 1987 was based on that very same proposal.

In the years between these two benchmarks, INF-related coverage followed a clear pattern of eventsism. That is, peaks or surges in the number of articles generally corresponded directly to major, officially sponsored events in the history of INF. The press could not be responsible for a given event if there was no evidence of a buildup in reporting before the event. So using eventsism as a test, one may conclude that the *Times* and the *Post* were mainly reflecting what was going on, not creating a particular environment or agenda.

Sources of information for the print press might also point to a certain level of dependence on the government. In the sample of the coverage from 1981 through 1987, U.S. government pronunciamento was the primary source of information for a majority of articles in four of the seven years. It appears in this context that a significant portion of the news might have been mainly a reflection of the administration's perspective.

According to the agenda-reflecting model, the press performs a transmitting function, relaying information from the government to the public. It follows that if this is the case, that information will most likely shine positively on administration policy. In 1983, an important year for both official plans for deployment of INF and negotiations with the Soviet Union in Geneva, articles that supported U.S. policy did represent a majority percentage of the overall coverage.

When the individual topics were grouped as to support, criticism, or neutrality vis-à-vis the government's handling of INF, neutral coverage predominated. In six of the seven years of the study, a majority percentage of *New York Times* articles were neutral on U.S. policy. This trend might indicate that the print media were simply describing what was going on at any given point. In this interpretation of these data on neutral reporting, the press was not adding spin or context but mostly transmitting information from the government to the public.

Level of Newspaper Coverage

Figure 18 shows that over the course of the seven-year period of INF, media coverage tended to focus on official events. It is not surprising that peaks in coverage related to specific events. The important point is that they were usually government-sponsored events. These findings might be used to support the notion that government action does set press behavior. This is exemplified by peaks in coverage at President Reagan's speech in November 1981, the Reagan-Gorbachev meeting at Reykjavik, the announcements of government proposals, and other events. All these peaks were government-driven and government-defined events. This general trend could be seen to reinforce the agenda-reflecting notion that the media react to events and do not stimulate them or provide leadership.[13]

That *New York Times* and *Washington Post* articles followed important events during the course of INF supports agenda-reflecting theory. The press cannot be dictating, setting, or building the official agenda when surges in the amount of coverage occur principally at the time an event is taking place. To affect the administration's INF program, a buildup in reporting would be evident in the data before a particular event or change in policy.

The Reagan administration's policy on INF remained consistent from the beginning to the end of the seven-year period. In 1981, the zero option was officially proposed by the U.S. government. The INF Treaty signed by the Soviet Union and the United States in 1987 was based on that same proposal. The point could be argued that neither the *New York Times* nor the *Washington Post* coverage of the INF process had any effect on the administration's agenda. After all, the data can be used to show that the print media acted as agenda-reflectors, serving as a conduit between the government and the public for information on official policy. The press did not change that policy; it simply reported that policy.

Sources of Information

The origination of the coverage might also point to the agenda-reflecting model. Figure 25 shows that identified U.S. government pronunciamento was the basis for a majority of *Times* and *Post* articles in four of seven years (1981, 1983, 1984, and 1987). Informational dependency is an important part of the agenda-reflecting model. One might also assume that the media are particularly encumbered on a national security issue such as arms control. The data hardly support the notion, however, that the print press was heavily dependent on the government for information. Alternative, nongovernment sources, though not supplying a consistent majority of the material, were an integral part of the coverage of INF.

A proponent of agenda-reflecting might still point, however, to data on the balance of sources from the *Times* and *Post*, shown in Figure 26. In six of seven years, a majority percentage of articles from the cross section examined cited only U.S. sources. The only year in which this trend was not present was 1983, when U.S. allies topped U.S. sources by 3 percent.

The data reveal that the press was relying on identified U.S. sources for a substantial percentage of information on INF. Also, articles from the *Times* and *Post* quoted these U.S. officials more frequently than any other source in six of seven years. These trends could be used to support the agenda-reflecting notion of media dependency. The press did rely on the administration as the most quotable source, which is some evidence to give a proponent of the agenda-reflecting model of press behavior something with which to argue a case.

Tone of INF Coverage

The next aspect of the analysis focuses on the actual content, or what the press was saying about INF and how it was saying it.

New York Times coverage from 1981 through 1987 was used for this analysis.

Figure 20 shows the breakdown of individual topics and the percentage of articles pertaining to each by year. In this breakdown, 1983 shows up as a particularly controversial year. This controversy might be attributed to specific events—the initiation of U.S. deployment of medium-range missiles in Europe and the Soviet walkout from the arms negotiations in Geneva. Despite these contentious events, agenda-reflectors could point out that the plurality (16 percent) of *New York Times* articles published on INF in that year supported the administration's policies. Such a pattern might indicate a press that was more reflecting than independent.

Individual topics were also grouped as to whether they could be considered supportive, critical, or neutral with regard to U.S. policy. Figure 21 illustrates the results of this categorization. The important point is that neutral articles accounted for a majority of the reporting in six of the seven years of the study.

In the agenda-reflecting model, the press simply conducts information from the government to the public. Because this model posits that the media do not inject any spin or context into the material, the high percentage of neutral coverage could indicate that the press was, indeed, transmitting hard information—not spin. This neutrality also might appear to contradict the notion that the print media were pursuing a separate agenda. Neutrality in tone implies acquiescence rather than advocacy.

According to the agenda-reflecting model, the government sets the political agenda. The media then act as a conduit from the administration to the public for information about official policy. The press is a dependent variable in this process, dependent on government sources for information and dependent on the administration for the agenda.

Some aspects of the analysis of *Times* and *Post* coverage can be used to support this agenda-reflecting tendency on the part of the press. The coverage did show a pattern of eventsism, surging at times when particular policies were enacted or events occurred. In this case, the print media primarily reported on government-defined and sponsored events, driven by the administration's agenda. Eventsism typifies agenda-reflecting because the press cannot affect the government or its policies if the bulk of its coverage occurs after government-sponsored events have taken place.

The press did, at times, follow officially sponsored events. Analysis of the *Times* showed that, even in a prestigious print source, reporting was largely neutral or objective. The print media were not necessarily incorporating individual context or pursuing a unique agenda. The data indicate that the coverage, for the most part, followed the administration's agenda and did so in a fairly objective fashion.

Given the nature of INF as an issue, this trend is not surprising. The majority of the information regarding INF, or any arms control issue, is in the hands of official sources. The confidentiality surrounding negotiations and other intergovernmental contact might also handicap the press. Data taken from the *Times* and the *Post* did confirm that U.S. government sources were most often cited in six of the seven years of the study. This information was then reported to the public in predominantly neutral tones in six of seven years. These patterns could be taken to support an agenda-reflecting theory of press behavior. But should they be? Do the data, in the main, really support the idea of a reflective print press?

Conclusions

The preceding sections discussing agenda-setting, agenda-building, and agenda-reflecting have emphasized the findings in the data that supported the basic premises of each theory. The vast amount of information involved in this study and the twists and turns found in the data make it difficult to draw definitive conclusions. Similar patterns exist both in print and in television, and some evidence appears stronger and more convincing. Let us consider both the general conclusions about the way the news media behave and the more particular conclusions as to how the two news media behave differently from each other.

Agenda-Setting

From an agenda-setting perspective, the *Times* and the *Post* coverage of INF could be characterized either as independent or as adversarial. That is, the press apparently reported independently of the administration's agenda, as well as government contacts. But it was also adversarial in its approach to covering official policy. Data from all three aspects of the analysis (overall coverage, topic focus in the *New York Times,* and in-depth analysis of the sample taken from both newspapers) could be interpreted to support these findings.

Levels of coverage from 1981 through 1987 show independence; the press focused on issues not consistent with the administration's INF agenda. The first surge in coverage in early 1981 marked the debate between the members of NATO over the deployment of medium-range missiles in Western Europe. Further, two notable peaks in 1982 correspond to the UN session on disarmament and state referenda in support of a nuclear freeze. Not only were the print media active in the amount of coverage during this early, formative phase of INF (1981 through 1983), but the newspapers also tended to focus on events that were not government-defined.

In fact, the data appear to indicate not only the independence of the print media but suggest a pro-arms-control bias. By focusing on issues not at all in concert with the administration's agenda, the media allowed for disproportionate attention to groups supporting these issues. The press was, at the very least, setting its own news agenda, putting arms control at the center of the INF controversy.

The *Times* and the *Post* used non-government-controlled sources most frequently in 1981 and 1982. Once again, these two years highlight the clear divergence between the administration's policies and agenda on INF and the content of the coverage. Alternative, nongovernment sources surpassed or equaled official U.S. sources in six of seven years. Government sources accounted for a greater percentage of origination only in 1987, primarily because of the INF Treaty in December of that year.

The high level of independence and activity in the media was supported by the type of articles that appeared in both the *Times* and the *Post*. News analysis represented a significant percentage of the overall coverage. Analytical coverage embodies both the independent and adversarial nature of the press in the agenda-setting theory. The *Times* and *Post* used a broad range of alternative information sources and showed the initiative to pursue aspects of INF that were not, at the time, part of the official agenda.

The adversarial relationship between the government and print media is the second part of the case for agenda-setting. A key element in the data pointing to agenda-setting is the high percentage of articles critical of administration policy in 1981. President Reagan did not announce the zero option until late November 1981. Although a dramatic surge in the number of *Times* and *Post* articles did occur at the time of the proposal, the high percentage of critical articles in 1981 cannot be attributed to this single event. Indeed, it is unlikely that a new arms control proposal to eliminate an entire class of nuclear weaponry would be received critically. What this trend highlights is the significant journalistic pressure for change in the administration's arms control policy before announcement of the zero option.

The adversarial nature of print reporting is evident throughout the early phase of INF. The percentages of articles critical of U.S. policy were highest in 1981 through 1983 and were greater than articles supportive of government policy in every year except 1985 and 1987. These two anomalies can be traced to the resumption of INF negotiations and the first Reagan-Gorbachev summit in 1985 and the treaty on INF in 1987.

As the negotiations took a more serious turn from 1985 through 1987, the coverage became predominantly neutral. *Times* and *Post* articles became less confrontational as the administration's policy of real arms control came on line.

It must be pointed out, however, that the *Times* and *Post* consistently printed more articles critical of the United States than critical of the Soviet Union. This might be attributed to the limited flow of information from the Soviet Union and the additional problem associated with language barriers. For whatever reason, however, the print press coverage was noticeably critical of official policy.

In what was being covered, news coverage from the first two years of the study, 1981 and 1982, indicates an independent press. The first surge in the number of articles for 1981 occurred during the debate in NATO over the deployment of INF in Western Europe. Further, the two peaks in coverage in 1982 were neither government-sponsored nor defined. Both events focused on issues or organizations outside the government's purview. Clearly, the *Times* and *Post* were independent during this period. And this early, formative phase in the life of an issue, according to the agenda-setting model, is the most important in affecting government policy.

In agenda-setting fashion, then, it appears the press was pushing for a change in U.S. policy on INF. The data suggest that the print media were more independent and adversarial than dependent and passive in covering INF.

Agenda-Building

The data also permit a case to be made for agenda-building. The most important evidence in favor of agenda-building is the way press activity generally reflects activity in the public sphere. Nongovernment groups and organizations were most active in the early stages of INF, and this activity was a focal theme in the media coverage. In the second half of the period, when this activity dropped off (1984–87), the press focused more on the government's agenda of events and policy.

Overall, the data show significant interplay between official policy and political agenda, public activity and agitation, and coverage of these aspects in the press. It appears that the print media reported and built on those aspects of INF that were not part of the government's agenda when the information was available. That is, during the initial phase of INF, 1981–83, nongovernment organizations were the most active, primarily in support of a more committed arms control agenda. Coverage of

INF in the *Times* and *Post* was, on average, both more extensive and varied during these first three years. Presumably, the press was able to build on the government's agenda because information from alternative, nongovernment sources was readily available, and nongovernment organizations were at their most active in opposing official policy. When these activities and alternative sources diminished from 1984 through 1987, however, the media turned to the government, reporting more on official events and policies. Correspondingly, coverage in these last four years became less critical of both administration policies and agenda on INF.

An argument could easily be made that, overall, the coverage in the *Times* and the *Post* supports an agenda-building model. Only one piece of data directly contradicts this supposition. Before President Reagan's announcement of the zero option, coverage of U.S. policy on INF was at its most critical. This criticism appeared before the agitation of nongovernment organizations in support of arms control and against the policy of deployment of medium-range missiles in Western Europe. This trend would suggest that the press was trying to do more than help build an agenda with regard to INF. Consequently, the independent and adversarial nature of the coverage during the next two years might be viewed as a case in agenda-setting reportage, rather than "mere" agenda-building.

Agenda-Reflecting

Data that support the agenda-setting or agenda-building models provide equally powerful arguments against the agenda-reflecting theory. Agenda-reflecting suggests that the media have no recourse but the official political agenda and serve simply as a conduit for information between the government and the public. As the term implies, the press reflects the official agenda and relies almost exclusively on government sources of information.

But only two patterns in the content data can be seen to support agenda-reflecting. First, there was a strong tendency in the press coverage toward eventsism. Except for the first two years of the period, 1981 and 1982, peaks in the number of articles corresponded directly to government-driven or defined events. This trend would indicate that the administration's agenda was the motivating force behind surges in coverage and that the media were reflecting that agenda. This piece of evidence is perhaps the strongest element in the case for agenda-reflecting.

A second argument in favor of the agenda-reflecting model is that the administration opened negotiations in 1981 with the zero option and finally signed an agreement in 1987 based on that proposal. This consistency might imply that the press had minimal or no impact on the official political agenda over the course of INF. This could be an important datum in favor of the agenda-reflecting theory. But the impetus and intent behind the original zero proposal must be examined.

Data on the level of criticism, support, and neutrality in *New York Times* coverage show that the majority of articles in 1981 were critical of the administration's handling of INF. This is the highest percentage of critical coverage in the seven-year period and the only year in which the percentage of either critical or supportive articles is higher than that of neutral.

This unfavorable coverage of government policy cripples the case for the agenda-reflecting model. In no way could a simply reflecting press take such an adversarial position with respect to the administration's agenda. In the end, although some agenda-reflecting patterns could be teased from these content data, the majority of the findings fit more closely with the agenda-setting and the agenda-building theories.

Comparison of Coverage: Television Versus Print

The data taken from print media have shown substantial support for agenda-setting, plausible support for agenda-building, and very little support for agenda-reflecting. But what might a comparison of print and television tell us about the applicability of each model?

Employing the same method of analysis used to examine the data individually, the first question requires a comparison of overall levels of coverage across the period 1981–87. Figures 15

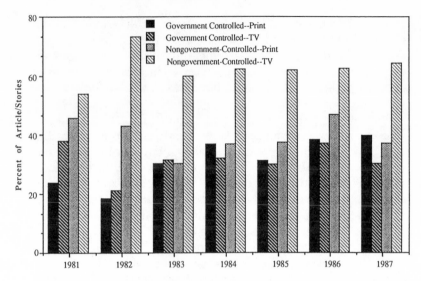

Fig. 27. Comparison of Origination for Print and Television Coverage of INF

and 18 leave a clear impression that electronic and print media parallel each other. Peaks from both sources occurred at the time of specific events.

This pattern of eventsism is, once again, the strongest point in the case for the agenda-reflecting model. The hole in this argument for a reflecting press, either print or electronic, is that several of the early peaks in coverage focused on non-government-sponsored events. In the strictest sense, if agenda-reflecting holds that the media serve only as a conduit for information from the government to the public, saturated coverage of events such as the UN disarmament session would refute that premise.

Both the agenda-building and agenda-setting models allow for non-government-sponsored coverage. The early focus on issues outside of the administration's agenda, as well as the high level of media activity in the first three years, 1981–83, could support either of these two theories. So at this point, it is fairly safe to rule out an application of the agenda-reflecting theory to either print or televised coverage of INF. Press behavior was clearly more than simply reflective of the official agenda.

The next step is to look at where the networks and print press were getting information. Figure 27 shows that non-government-controlled sources dominated the origination of network coverage throughout the period. Data on the sources of newspaper coverage indicate a much more equal use of government and nongovernment sources in all but the first two years of the study, 1981 and 1982.

The question, then, is whether the networks were more independent in their reporting than the *Times* and *Post*. According to a narrow interpretation of the data on origination, the answer would appear to be that they were.

Other factors, however, must also be considered in this evaluation. The print press is generally more balanced in the sources it uses because reporters have more time and space to devote to a story. Networks, conversely, tend to have only a short time (often measured in seconds) in which to deliver a story. Televised press would also be more likely to gravitate to those sources providing the most dramatic soundbites in an attempt to attract more viewers. An antinuclear rally, for example, would be more visually interesting than the administration's latest press release.

The origination or sources of information used by both networks and newspapers could be used to support either the agenda-setting or agenda-building models of press behavior. The high percentage of network stories based on nongovernment information would appear to indicate a highly independent press and an agenda-setting pattern. The more balanced sourcing evident in the print press would tend to indicate the agenda-building model.

More important than where the media were getting information on INF is the question of how that information was presented to the public. From the tone of the coverage, it is clear that the print press was much more independent-minded than the networks and often took an adversarial position vis-à-vis administration policy. The number of articles inherently crit-

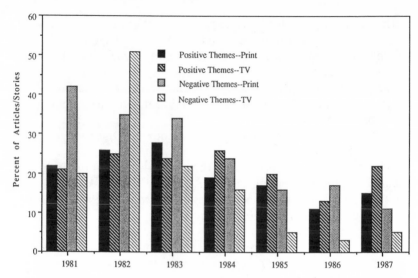

Fig. 28. Comparison of Positive and Negative Themes in Print and Television Coverage of INF

ical of the official U.S. position surpassed those that were inherently supportive in five of seven years of the study, 1981–84 and 1986. Figure 28 shows that the electronic media were not nearly so contentious in their reporting; levels of critical coverage were higher than supportive in only one year, 1982.

At this point, we must also add a corollary about the independence of the networks in 1982. The networks naturally focused most on those aspects of INF that provided the best visual impact. The European protests and antinuclear demonstrations in the United States were at their height in 1982, providing much greater visual interest than "talking heads" at the negotiations. These events, which provided readily available visuals, allowed television to report on INF with an *appearance*—not necessarily the *reality*—of greater independence.

Comparison of these data leads to some interesting conclusions about both press behavior as it relates to the negotiation process and the nature of print versus television coverage as a whole. In the case of INF, network news presents a clearer agenda-building pattern—saturation reporting on topics relevant to the official agenda. The high level of activity surrounding the European protests and nuclear freeze movement created a surge of coverage by the networks in 1982 that was critical of administration policy. But these events provided the exciting visual interest television prefers, creating a brief illusion of independence. Overall, electronic press behavior fits in nicely with the agenda-building model.

The print press demonstrates a stronger agenda-setting tendency—more independent and adversarial, as well as analytical and investigation-oriented, than television. The aspect that illustrates this pattern more clearly than any other is the high percentage of articles that were critical of official policy on INF in 1981. This criticism was evident before the administration's announcement of the double zero proposal. This early negative coverage by the print media gives a good indication of an independent press actually driving the political agenda. A case can be made that the *Times* and the *Post*—both important news sources among the political elite—actually pressured the administration into adding arms control—double zero—to the INF agenda.

The content data provide a clear picture of the overall difference between print and electronic press. The elite press—*New York Times* and *Washington Post*—is significantly more adversarial in its behavior than the broadcast news media. Print apparently acts like an agenda-setter; network news acts more like an agenda-builder.

Analysis of content data alone, however, cannot tell us which medium, if any, really affected the process. To what degree do government officials pay attention to what is going on in the press—or, conversely, try to influence reporting? How great a role do journalists play in either setting or building on the official agenda? These questions address the critical issue of press impact.

Interviews with both journalists and government officials involved with the INF process are essential to a complete understanding of the more subjective query into media impact. These interviews provide an insider perspective on the relationship between administration officials and members of the press and how they view both one another's and their own role in the arms control process. So the question still remains, Do the media have a real and palpable impact on the political agenda, or on the people that set that agenda, or, for that matter, on the public?

The People

CHAPTER 5

The Journalists' Perspective

There is a deep down structural conflict between the
press and the government. . . . The press is in the
business of finding out secrets, the government is in
the business of keeping them, and each is just doing
their own job.

—Anonymous journalist

The chapters in Part I described what the media
were actually reporting on INF. The content analysis provided
hard evidence about our first two questions relating to "newswork," that is, where the news media got information on INF
and how they presented that information to the public.

In Part II, the focus shifts from quantitative to qualitative
evidence—from data about news coverage to interviews with
journalists who reported the news on INF and officials who
were involved in the policymaking and negotiating processes.
Information from these interviews is designed to complement
the content analysis by corroborating findings on the "where"
and "how" questions of press coverage and providing more insights into newswork and questions of press impact as well.

This chapter focuses on what journalists perceived their news
product—and their role within the political process of INF—to
be. The first section compares findings from the content analysis with the views of reporters themselves about how (or how
well) they did their job. Although readdressing these issues
might seem redundant, it is important to determine whether
the people writing or presenting the news agree with my findings about their coverage.

The second half of the chapter is devoted to journalists' views
of their own influence and impact on INF policy and the negotiations. That section focuses on what journalists had to say

about their role in INF and how that role might be classified. It looks, too, at whether these views support or contradict the concluding impression from the content analysis of the agenda-influencing nature of press behavior.

Checking the Content Analysis

A fundamental question addressed in the content analysis and examined in these interviews concerns where the press gets its information. Reporters discussed what they believed to be their best sources and how they used those sources either for corroboration or to encourage another source to speak more freely.[1]

Dateline Washington

Reporters generally agreed with the content findings about the *where* of newswork. Most of the official information on the INF negotiations came not from Geneva, where the negotiations were being held, but from Washington, D.C. Jeffrey Smith of the *Washington Post* characterized the atmosphere in Geneva as a "cone of silence."[2] Other front-line reporters confirmed this notion and justified their practice at the same time. One reporter stated that many people in Washington are knowledgeable about what is going on and "aren't particularly restrained from talking about it."

Reporters considered these Washington contacts vital sources of information and tended to disdain the official releases distributed by government agencies and press offices in Washington. One journalist, known for his work on the arms control process, said that "the official press releases were ludicrously uninformative." He went on to say that these official statements, as a whole, "tended to be, if not obfuscatory, at least not very forthcoming."

Avoiding Government "Spin Doctors"

Reporters generally viewed these government releases as uninformative, as well as carefully crafted to present the administration's INF policy and progress in the negotiations in the best light possible. Reporter Jeffrey Smith of the *Post* speaks directly to that political reality:

If a negotiator had his way, what we would write about is enormous public policy successes and that the United States government acted monolithically to approve or disapprove certain policy decisions. They [U.S. proposals] were all accepted by the Soviet Union, and, as a consequence, we got a treaty with all the provisions in it that we wanted, and we didn't have to give up anything.[3]

All of the journalists interviewed said that the government tried to put its spin on the news, hoping to give official INF policy or the negotiations the proverbial "rosy glow." One reporter, when asked if officials tried to create a mood or feeling in the press, simply replied, "Constantly." David Martin rounded out this comment, adding, "The government tries to put a spin on everything."[4]

The government, however, was far from monolithic in its views of INF, and it had no corner on the opinion market. The press avoided the official spin by using as many sources as possible. Journalists did consider people within various government agencies and the executive branch, as well as congressional staff, important sources of information. But the press corps also relied on people who worked in and around Washington, were not currently in government service, or were members of nongovernment organizations.[5]

Cultivating a Dialogue

Reporters who cover issues such as arms control or other areas of national security often try to develop a dialogue with these sources. The source—whether inside or outside the administration—provides information to the journalist, and the journalist frequently offers some perspective or piece of information that the individual had not previously considered. Talking with different sources, who were both part of and removed from government, and using this dialogue was generally viewed by journalists as the best way to get at "the truth."

This system of verification was often used when reporters received information from Soviet or Eastern European sources. One reporter recalled being approached during the INF negotiations by East European diplomats, who were usually operating under instructions. Whenever that occurred, the journalist would use the information provided to ask questions of American sources, indicating that the story had originated from the Eastern bloc. Both sides would then be used in the article. According to the reporter, these stories generally turned out to be accurate and were often precursors to positions taken formally in the negotiations themselves.

This method supports the findings on origination from the content analysis. The analysis showed that the media did not depend on the government as the sole source of either information or expertise. The data also support, however, the premise that journalists did not ignore what government insiders had to say. Indeed, the press appears to have developed a system of its own for extracting and cross-checking information from official channels.

The System: Backgrounders and Leaks

Multiple sources were commonly used in media coverage of INF, creating a system of checks and balances. The journalist checked information between sources and also tended to employ information gained from one source to encourage another source to speak more freely. In this system, reporters frequently used conditions of "background" during their interviews. Background conditions provide the source with anonymity and, in so doing, encourage a source to divulge information that he or she might otherwise be reluctant to discuss. These conditions varied somewhat, depending on the reporter and on the individual being interviewed, but the basic reality remained: backgrounding allowed journalists to obtain news and information that they might not have uncovered otherwise.[6]

At times, these restrictions created an opportunity for government officials to manipulate the press. Anonymity encourages a source to disclose more facts but can also be used to promote an alternative policy or cast aspersions on policy or strategy with impunity. Administration officials could thereby manipulate coverage to their own advantage without jeopardizing their position.

Walter Pincus of the *Washington Post* believed that government officials often tried to advance a specific agenda using the press. "If you're a reporter and someone in government is talking to you about classified information, you're a fool if you think they're doing it out of friendship or out of ego. They're doing it because they think it's the right thing for their own purposes."[7]

One reporter who had numerous and close contacts within the bureaucracy said that these "leaks" became standard operating procedure because of the contentious nature of the INF issue.

Leaks are instruments of bureaucratic warfare that goes on, and particularly went on, during the Reagan administration. I had the most success getting people to talk when the government was most divided over what policy should be. I could go back and forth between the different camps. The leak becomes something that is beneficial both to the leaker and the leakee.[8]

Nearly all the reporters interviewed for this study shared this view that leaks and backgrounders were, on balance, beneficial and that those leaks and backgrounders did not render reporters powerless to withstand manipulation.

Reporters did believe, however, that getting information under these conditions put an extra burden on them to make certain they had more than one source on which to build a story, especially on controversial issues. One reporter believed that, in these cases, multiple sourcing was important both to the story and, in the long term, to a journalist's reputation. "The reporter's reputation and his ability to serve his reader are based on getting enough information to judge and interpret that information, so whatever the motivation of the source, he is not being used."[9] This reporter went on to confirm that multiple sourcing, knowledge about the issue, and judgment were key to avoiding manipulation.[10]

The data, too, showed that both electronic and print media relied on a combination of government and nongovernment sourcing. Interviews with journalists augment these findings, indicating that reporters did, indeed, use a combination of sources in putting together their stories. The quantitative evidence could not show, however, that reporters sometimes had to work harder when using government contacts to sidestep efforts by officials to manipulate the coverage.

As a corollary to this issue, it appears that print journalists had greater opportunity to cross-check and verify material from different contacts. Television journalists generally attributed this to print reporters having more time to do investigative research. David Martin of CBS said that, in the electronic media, by the time you "ferret out" information this way, it has become a "marginal television story." Accordingly, one might assume that such time restraints would render television journalists more susceptible to manipulation by government and nongovernment interests.

Overall, with regard to the general "where" question of news origination, the interviews support the findings from the content analysis and supply some interesting insights. One such insight revealed first that Washington was command central for the media. If a reporter wanted information on INF policy or even the negotiations in Geneva, Washington was the place to find that information.

Second, the content analysis indicated that a significant percentage of coverage originated from government sources. Journalists confirmed and augmented this notion, saying that these contacts were valuable in keeping them informed on the policy and process of INF. What reporters also revealed, however, and what the content analysis could not tell, was their system for checking sources. Different sources within the administration often reflected diverse opinions about INF policy and strategy. Reporters would use this diversity to extract additional information from sources and combine that information with material from sources outside the bureaucracy. Both the quantitative analysis and the qualitative evidence from these interviews showed that the press relied on multiple sources, balancing official information with material from alternative, nongovernment sources.

Press behavior with respect to the origin of information on INF seems to support the notion of media independence. When using government—and presumably nongovernment—sources, reporters were aware of the need to corroborate and cross-check the information they received. This practice could be used to support an argument for either the agenda-building or agenda-setting models.

A Press with a Cause?

It is fairly safe to make an initial assumption in addressing the issue of how the press presented information on INF and the general tone of the coverage. Reporters approached INF, or would approach any issue, with their own opinions and viewpoints. These preconceptions could, in turn, affect the tone of coverage on any given issue.[11]

Overwhelmingly, when asked about their own news product, reporters responded that they were simply trying to find out what was going on and report it without injecting personal views. The slogan among journalists when asked about the coverage of INF policy and process was, "We don't make the news, we just report it."

This was fairly standard ideology among press interviewees—that they, as a group, report only what is going on and do not themselves make, create, or influence the news. This ideology might tend to blind many reporters to the impact of their own predilections on context, bias, and, ultimately, news product.

In discussing this possibility, one journalist conceded that, as a group, the press does have predictable political leanings.

A significant majority of the journalists who cover international security affairs and who have access both to broad and elite audiences tend toward the liberal end of the spectrum. . . . That means the line, the impression people are going to get . . . will come from that vantage point. Particularly in foreign policy and national security, the center of gravity of that quite diverse group is *definitely on the liberal side.*[12]

The content analysis suggested a tendency in the media to favor a pro-arms-control agenda with respect to INF. It would be overly simplistic to say, however, that the high percentage of negative coverage directed at the Reagan administration's policy from 1981 through 1983 was a result of the liberal agenda of those doing the reporting.[13]

It would be equally incorrect to assume that the press's political bias—"definitely on the liberal side"—had no effect on the tone of the coverage. Indeed, as before, content analysis and quotations from journalists reinforce the basic point—the coverage and the coverers both tilted somewhat toward a liberal, pro-arms-agreement perspective.

Evidence from *New York Times* editorials and commentaries could be used to support this notion of a liberal press bias. In every year except for 1987, when the INF Treaty was signed, articles of this type that were inherently critical of U.S. policy far surpassed the percentage of those that supported the administration. This pattern is important in terms of press bias because editorials and commentaries generally represent the views of the journalistic community.

Some of the reporters did say that they originally believed that the Reagan administration, upon taking office in 1981, had no intention of promoting arms control as a serious part of its foreign policy. Most reporters interviewed (75 percent) also gave the clear impression that, looking back, they wished Reagan had been more serious in this regard from the outset.

The Reagan administration failed in what was their original intent, which was to drive a spike through the heart of arms control. . . . Arms control survived, in part because . . . the press conveyed the widespread preferences of the body politic, and believed, as a matter of editorial opinion, that the administration was misguided.[14]

The content analysis supports the notion that the press, and the news establishment as a whole, preferred arms control. The high percentage of negative coverage of official INF policy during the first three years of the period, 1981 through 1983, could be used to argue that the press was biased against the administration's policy. That policy was considered "misguided," as one reporter characterized it.

The content analysis also showed that INF coverage in the *New York Times* was most inherently critical of administration policy in 1981. The zero proposal was not announced until the end of November 1981 and would not have contributed to the trend toward critical coverage. From what journalists have said about early U.S. policy on INF, we might attribute this trend to the Reagan government's early pursuit of deployment and apparent lack of strategy with respect to arms control. If the press did believe that this policy was misguided, criticism of the administration's actions was a way to communicate that message.

When the zero option was presented in late 1981, journalists generally viewed the proposal, not as a serious offer, but as a political maneuver by the government to allay the concerns of critics and smooth the path for deployment.[15] David Martin captured the sentiment of many reporters when he characterized the zero option proposal as proof that the Reagan administration was "not serious about arms control." Because the press did not believe the administration's commitment to reach an agreement was credible, a significant percentage of the coverage of U.S. policy over the next two years, 1982–83, continued to be negative.[16]

Reporters did tend to admit that they were slightly biased in favor of arms control. But these responses also provide a more subtle indicator that journalists were aware of their own independence in the news process. Many reporters seemed to understand the importance of context, slant, and perception of the news with respect to policymaking.

I think the Reagan administration was worried about the perception [in the press] that it was just opposed on principle to any arms control negotiations and was doing nothing but being obstructionist. To the extent they were worried, they addressed the [arms control] issue seriously.[17]

Journalists, on balance, confirmed trends found in the content analysis. The press was more involved and more of a player in INF than the agenda-reflecting model allows. As the content data suggested, agenda-building cannot be ruled out as a possibility in describing press behavior. Evidence from reporters themselves on their sources of information and the way they presented that information, however, points more to an agenda-setting form of journalism.

Assessing the Role of the Press

Quantitative evidence from the content analysis and qualitative support from the interviews show that the press was independent both in where it got information on INF and how it presented that information in its news product. A minority (38 percent) tended to support the notion that how they presented INF might have been influenced by a general press bias in favor of arms control.

We now turn to how journalists viewed their role in the INF process. Apparently, the role of the press in reporting on government policy and policymaking goes beyond simply reporting facts and events. Indeed, the media were an important means of communication and expression for those inside and outside of the bureaucracy.

The role of the press, however, seems to have extended well beyond communicating news and information. This very positioning of the press—as it relayed ideas and information among those in power—seems to have created an additional role—called here "press as respondent." Evidence from the interviews indicates the media were both communicating and responding to ideas about INF policy and strategy.

Press as "Interoffice" Communicator

Journalists believed that government officials relied on the press, particularly the *New York Times* and *Washington Post*, to let others know, and to find out for themselves, what was going on. One reporter summed up this idea, saying, "In a democracy, the press is a source for legislators and the public to view what people in government are doing." Reporters and their news organizations "select the sights and sounds"[18] that people in Washington will read, hear, and discuss. "Government officials understand that one of the ways you garner support for policy is to start with the press because, as journalists, we're part of the food chain on disseminating information."[19] The media are an important part of that "food chain," and journalists agreed that the spread of information is a substantial part of their function.

This role of press as communicator was important in the case of INF. Different branches of government often had different views about policy and negotiating strategy. The press, in this instance, served as a means for different parts of the bureaucracy—and other interested parties—to communicate.

Because of divisions within the administration over policy and negotiating issues, the media also acted as a forum for political debate. Reporters found that they—and their reporting—were often a battleground between different branches of government, departments, and other groups. "There's no doubt we became the vehicles through which government people got their stories across—those who wanted to influence the negotiations in one way or another."[20]

The press was the vehicle. But because evidence forcefully suggests press bias favoring arms control, could the press itself have attempted to influence the political debate, even the policy at issue? That is, while serving as a means for various parties to communicate their views and as a forum in which to air these views, might the press itself have become a participant?

The answer is yes: media participation in the debate over INF policy is presented here through the theory of "press as respondent."

Press as Respondent

As a matter of editorial opinion, the media were generally biased in favor of arms control and apparently expressed that view in their coverage, responding both to the INF issue and U.S. policy. For example, the quantitative data suggest that when the administration appeared less committed to arms control, press coverage was more critical. Conversely, when the administration seemed to pursue an agreement more vigorously, coverage became less critical. The press followed the issue closely and was evidently able to participate in the political debate.

Both quantitative and qualitative evidence indicates that the media were interested in the INF issue, particularly the debate over policy. Jeffrey Smith of the *Post* believed these conflicts were the most significant aspect of the coverage. "The divisions within the administration were the biggest part of what was actually happening. . . . The story of the INF . . . was a story of conflict between people who had different views."[21]

The amount of coverage devoted to INF supports press interest in the policy debate and serves as an indicator of just how important the media believed this issue to be. The policymaking and negotiating processes were the subjects of intense media attention and scrutiny. Thousands of newspaper articles and television minutes were devoted to INF. But did press interest simply reflect public interest—is it actually public opinion, not press opinion, that government officials must persuade and to which they appeal?

The evidence suggests that the American public took little interest in the INF issue. A poll taken less than a week before the INF Treaty was signed showed that 72 percent of Americans knew little or nothing about the issue.[22] Reporters apparently knew they were playing to a fairly limited audience. David Ensor of ABC said, "There wasn't a significant degree of interest in the public on INF."[23]

This trend supports studies that have found that public attitudes do not generally reflect a great deal of knowledge about the details of arms control. With respect to INF, specifically, one survey conducted in January 1988 found that fully 34 percent of the public, when asked three questions about INF, did not know any of the answers. Most of the remaining interviewees made incorrect guesses.[24] These data are particularly revealing because the INF Treaty between the United States and the Soviet Union was signed only one month before the survey and was accompanied by considerable media fanfare.

Overall, the American public was largely uninterested in and unaware of the specifics of arms control and INF. The press was also somewhat removed from the pulse of public opinion on INF. David Martin characterized Washington journalism as a "closed circle"—reporters often did not follow what was printed or televised beyond the major newspapers and networks. This separation would tend to make it more difficult for the media either to understand or to represent mass public opinion or beliefs.

And this nonopinion is one of the principal justifications—if not the major justification—for not looking closely at the impact of news on public opinion. Indeed, the nonopinions of the public formed the main indicator of what role the press was playing. That role was to respond.

The findings from quantitative and qualitative evidence appear to support the notion of press as respondent. The lack of public interest, the limited contact of the press with mainstream, mass public opinion, and the attentiveness of the media to the INF issue all indicate that the public debate was actually a press debate. In discussing the influence of the mass media on public attitudes, one scholar suggested that "the media *are* public opinion."[25] The case can be made that, with respect to INF, the press could have served as a representative or surrogate public opinion.

The way reporters selected, prioritized, presented, and even responded to issues and policies was guided and shaped by their own core values and beliefs. The question remains, however, What impact did press role and press bias have on the policymaking and negotiating process in the context of the three models of press behavior?

Impact and Models of Press Behavior

Journalists were universally uncomfortable in addressing the question of their own impact on the policymaking and negotiating processes. It is likely that government officials, who formulated and worked with policy on a daily basis, were in a better position to judge, or, at least, to admit to the press's impact.[26] Nonetheless, reporters' responses both to direct and indirect questions about impact provide some clues about press influence and behavior. These impressions about the impact of the media, in conjunction with the findings from the "where" and "how" questions, will enable us to assess press behavior in the context of the three models.

Agenda-Reflecting

The agenda-reflecting theory suggests that the press does not have an impact on official policy or policymaking and is dependent in its relationship with the government. That is, reporters are dependent on officials for information and serve only as a conduit for that information from the government to the public. According to the agenda-reflecting model, the press puts no spin on, and provides little or no nongovernment context to, the news product.

Only 25 percent of the journalists interviewed said either that the press had no impact or that it was impossible to determine what its impact was. Unfortunately for proponents of the agenda-reflecting model, these same reporters also pointed out in more indirect discussion that the media had affected policy or the negotiations in some fashion.

Walter Pincus was part of this minority, saying, "The only . . . people who can judge the impact are the people who are doing the negotiating." Although Pincus refused to speculate about the specifics of press impact, he later admitted that the media were "very important" and, at certain times, "played a serious role."[27]

Though reluctant to admit to or discuss impact per se, journalists described a behavior that was more than simply reflecting the official agenda. First, in gathering information, reporters relied on varied and diverse sources, both inside and outside the bureaucracy. Also, when government sources were used as part of a story, journalists developed a system for corroborating and balancing that information. According to reporters, material, opinion, or expertise from alternative sources, government and nongovernment, were used to ensure the credibility of the news product.

Reporters were independent both in gathering the news and in the way they presented that news. The agenda-reflecting model suggests that the press simply transmits information from official sources. Both the content analysis and the interviews with reporters, however, show a discernible press bias in the coverage of INF favoring a more vigorous commitment to arms control than the Reagan administration initially demonstrated.

One reporter acknowledged that the press participated in the movement to pressure the administration to take action toward arms control. If this was the case, the press was not merely transmitting information or reflecting the official agenda.

The notion of press as communicator might imply a passive role for the media, more in keeping with the agenda-reflecting model of press behavior, that is, a role of simply communicating or transmitting information. The diverse sources of information that were used, however, and the possible influence of press bias suggest that what might appear to be a passive role was actually more independent in nature.

The idea of press as respondent in the case of INF further indicates that the press was at least an interactive, if not a fully independent, player in the political debate. The lack of public interest in INF and attentiveness to the issue among the press strengthen the argument that public debate could actually have become press debate.

Despite reporters' unwillingness to address the question of impact directly, their responses to the "where" and "how" questions of press behavior, combined with data from the content analysis, indicate a fairly independent press. The agenda-reflecting model does not explain the patterns of behavior found here.

Agenda-Building

The agenda-building model states that the press gathers information from a variety of sources, government and nongovernment. Journalists then integrate this material to provide framework, context, and detail to their news product. In this way, the press can influence the context of an issue and thereby may help to shape public perceptions of government policy. According to the agenda-building model, the public in turn affects policy through its reaction.

Evidence from the content analysis and interviews with journalists indicate that the press frequently availed itself of various sources of information about INF, both government and nongovernment. The media presented this information in what might be described as an interactive fashion. That is, the press interacted with the material, providing context and spin about INF policy that was often, though not always, critical of administration strategy.

Evidence from both of these aspects of press behavior could be used to support the agenda-building model. Proponents of agenda-building argue, again, that it is the public through its reaction, not the press, that has an impact on government policy. The press contributes to this impact only inasmuch as it provides the public with the information on which to make a judgment. Public pressure, according to the agenda-building theory, influences government policy.

Journalists were reluctant to discuss the question of impact. One might assume, though, from their ideology of simply reporting the news, and not creating it, that they might agree that it is the public that influences official policy and that they contribute only by arming the public with information from various and diverse sources.

Walter Pincus commented, however, that he believed it was not the general public that was most interested in what the press had to say. "We were trying to keep track of what was going on in serious foreign policy and arms control issues. The people who are most interested are the people involved—up on the Hill and in the bureaucracy."[28]

Indeed, survey data on public knowledge about INF, gathered in January 1988, just after the treaty was signed, seem to confirm this notion—or at least indicate that the American public was not attuned to the INF issue. Without public awareness, it is unlikely that there was public participation to any significant degree, much less demands for change in U.S. foreign policy. And without public action or drive for change in government policy on INF, the agenda-building model—which places the press in the middle of the policy process—falls short in describing press or public behavior.

Agenda-Setting

The agenda-setting model is similar to the agenda-building model in suggesting that reporters use government and nongovernment sources in their investigations. Here the similarity ends, however, because according to the agenda-setting model, the press can be considered independent in the issues it selects, as well as how it presents them. Proponents of agenda-setting believe the media have the ability to put issues on the political agenda and affect the course of government policy.

Evidence on the "where" question with respect to INF supports the agenda-setting notion of the press's independent sourcing. Nongovernment sources were frequently used. Opposing views within the administration also made regular appearances in the pages of major newspapers or during nightly news broadcasts.

On the question of how the press presented this material on INF, both quantitative and qualitative evidence indicated press bias, suggesting that the press could have been pursuing an independent agenda. This bias centered around a conviction that arms control was necessary.

Drawing an analogy to that conviction, quantitative data from the content analysis on criticism or support for government policy in the press coverage can be seen as an "applause meter." When the arms control process was most threatened by official plans to deploy medium-range weapons in Europe in 1981, critical coverage predominated in the print press. When the administration demonstrated a greater commitment to negotiating, negative coverage gradually dropped off, and the needle on the meter began to swing in a more supportive direction.

Most of the journalists conceded that they might, indeed, have acted as agents for change with respect to arms control and INF. One reporter believed that the Reagan government had "every intention of killing off arms control in 1981 . . . but the press, as part of a larger movement, pressured the administration to change and the zero option was created."[29]

Here we cross the line between press bias—which refers to how an issue is presented—and pressure for change—which implies a more direct impact of press behavior and the press. Apparently, reporters were aware that they were pressuring policymakers in an attempt to influence the political agenda.

David Ensor felt the amount of attention INF received and the pressure this created did have an impact on the negotiations, reminiscent of Ranney's theory of "fast-forwarding": "If an issue is getting a lot of attention from the media, that increases the pressure on the negotiators to achieve results in less time."[30]

Ensor was supported by a fellow journalist who believed the press had an impact on INF "because it established the atmosphere of tolerance—patience or impatience—in which the negotiators had to work."[31]

Television coverage might have had a special impact on this atmosphere. David Martin of CBS felt that arms control as an issue did not lend itself to television coverage because it lacked visual appeal. INF established an unusual precedent in this regard because both the European protests and the freeze movement were well-suited to graphic television portrayal and made INF more accessible to the electronic press.[32] Pressure from the media, at least from 1981 through 1983, apparently came from a combination of print and television coverage.

But did this coverage and associated political pressure have a discernible impact on either policymaking or the negotiations? In his book, Strobe Talbott attributes chief negotiator Paul Nitze's attempted 1982 compromise, the "walk in the woods," to these almost daily reports of European domestic opposition both in the press and on television. "Nitze was [concerned] that failure to reach agreement would be far more costly to the West than to the Soviet Union, since European popular opposition to deployment in the absence of an agreement could traumatize and perhaps paralyze the alliance for years to come."[33]

Nor were the Soviets, according to one journalist, above trying to use pressure in (and by) the Western media to their own advantage in the negotiations. "The Soviets were using [coverage of the protests] constantly as a stick to beat the Americans over the head with. The Americans were constantly reminded that if the deployment went ahead as scheduled, there was going to be opposition."[34]

The press's role as a communicator made it particularly effective as a lobby pressuring for arms control. Journalists recognized their role in the spread of information, especially within the U.S. policymaking and power structure. This role takes on an important additional meaning if the press itself was trying to pressure or influence the political agenda, and, as a means of communication, the media were in a position to do so—as respondent.

This new role is presented here as press as respondent. That is, the press was communicating ideas about INF and, because of its own biases, worldview, and opinions, was also participating in the policy debate. The press participated directly through opinion expressed in editorials and commentaries and indirectly in what it chose to cover and emphasize. This notion was not confirmed by reporters themselves, but they did acknowledge some press bias with respect to INF.

Although reluctant to discuss their impact directly, journalists did provide some interesting insights about their news product and its possible consequences. This evidence confirmed findings from the content analysis about where the press was getting information on INF and how it then presented that information. Taken together with interviews of major journalists, this evidence defines the press as a policy respondent—not as a policy vehicle.

CHAPTER 6

Officially Speaking

There was an enormous amount of press interest and
press pressure on us [the negotiators]. . . . The INF
issue had become so hyper-political that we couldn't
remove ourselves from that. The public dimension
had become *the* dimension—had become the essence
of the issue, as opposed to the internal negotiations
themselves. *It was really a battle for the press.*

The most striking impression gleaned from interviews with government officials was the degree to which
they were conscious of the press. Officials were aware of the
utility of the press in explaining and garnering support for policies and programs, as well as the power of press in evaluating
those policies and programs.

Both senior and junior officials involved in INF highlighted
the importance of the press as a way to "get the message out."
Officials and journalists recognized that the media, electronic
and print, were the primary vehicle for the government to present and defend its position.

Government officials provide a unique perspective on the
three questions selected to help define press behavior in the case
of INF. With regard to the question of where the press got its
information, officials expressed their views about the relative
dependence of the press on the government for information, as
well as the interplay of backgrounders and leaks between press
and policymakers. Were these anonymous interviews a way for
people inside the administration to manipulate the press? Or
were reporters as successful as they believed in avoiding manipulation and using backgrounders to uncover "the truth"?

On the question of how the press presented information,
officials involved in INF had strong opinions with respect to the
tone of the coverage and press bias. These opinions fell into

three general categories. First, the press seemed overeager for an agreement. Second, the media focused too much attention on the debate within the administration, which, according to officials, made the coverage "sensational." Finally, officials believed the press overemphasized the political dimension of INF—liberal versus conservative, Congress versus the executive, and so on. These views on the tone of INF coverage will be discussed and compared with evidence both from the content analysis and the interviews with journalists.

We will then explore what this information reveals about the role of the press. Did officials support the characterizations of press as communicator and press as respondent? Did the administration develop a specific strategy to deal effectively with either or both of these press functions?

Finally, after looking at press role as both communicator and respondent, we will address again the issue of press impact, referring to the three models—agenda-setting, agenda-building, and agenda-reflecting.

Officials' Thoughts on Press Origination

Evidence from the content analysis and interviews with journalists indicated that the press, though using government sources, was by no means dependent on those sources. Alternative sources made up a significant percentage of the origination of media coverage of INF.

Independent Sourcing and the Press's System

Government officials generally supported this evidence, saying the media were not dependent on either negotiators or officials for information. When government sources were used by the press, officials also confirmed what reporters had said about their system for gathering information.

The most industrious reporters have a wide range of sources that they carefully play off against each other. They try to have a very broad base of sources, which tends to give redundancy and cuts down on the possibility of error. [Multiple sourcing] also allows them to start with something very small and develop it.[1]

These remarks from James Timbie, technical adviser to the INF negotiating team and technical expert for the Arms Control and Disarmament Agency (ACDA), typified the attitude of most officials and supports what journalists themselves said about their system for gathering information. Reporters routinely shuttled between different branches of government to corroborate information or elicit alternate opinions. Such a modus operandi would explain why government sources provided a consistent percentage of press origination in the content analysis.

Not all of the officials agreed, however, with the idea of independent sourcing in the media. Kenneth Adelman, director of ACDA for much of the INF period, believed that most of the press's information on INF came from official sources. This view contradicts findings from the content analysis, statements by journalists, and the opinions of most of the other officials who were interviewed. Only Richard Perle, former assistant secretary of defense, offered weak support for Adelman's claim on media sourcing, but he immediately qualified his remark.

Ultimately, the press is dependent on the government for information. Although, if people talked to that community of experts outside of government, it was sometimes easier for the press to pick up stuff from them—people close to but not directly involved in the negotiations.[2]

Perle's remark does not contradict the finding from the content analysis that a significant, though by no means exclusive, percentage of press coverage relied on official information. Even journalists admitted to using administration and bureaucratic sources frequently for material. There are two important issues here. First, alternative sources were a part of press origination. And second, when official sources were involved, journalists and most officials agreed that the press had an effective system for cross-checking and corroborating that information.

Backgrounder or Leak

These exchanges—the dialogue—between officials and reporters commonly took place under conditions of "background" or "deep background." When asked to explain these conditions, Max Kampelman, chief negotiator for the INF talks, specified that to the Geneva negotiating team deep background meant no attribution and no Geneva dateline on the resulting article. Most of his talking, Kampelman added, was carried out under these guidelines because he was hoping for greater understanding of the situation by reporters, rather than publicity for himself. He used these backgrounders when it was necessary to convey information to the public for influence, persuasion, and credibility.

[In Geneva] we were looking to promote greater understanding for our positions. We used backgrounders, at times, to be even specific about what was going on in the negotiations. Sometimes when you did that, you were, perhaps, technically in violation of the confidentiality agreement between the U.S. and Soviet negotiating teams. So, by having the "no dateline, no attribution," you put a wall in between you and the story.[3]

Kampelman refused to characterize these episodes as "leaks." "It's wrong to call it a leak. It's just that the government can choose when it wishes to issue information at a time and place of its own choosing. Rightfully so, I think."[4]

According to officials, there was a fine line, often crossed during the INF process, between productive backgrounders and controversial leaks. Generally, differentiating between the two was a subjective call. When it advanced their own particular agenda, officials did not consider passing information to the media leaking. If the information ran counter to their objectives, however, it was deemed a leak. Regardless of the terminology, officials evidently used this system and, in turn, served as a source of information for the press.

Washington Speaks Easy

Nearly all the officials interviewed agreed that Washington rather than Geneva was the source of leaks to the press on INF. James Timbie pointed out that, at times, an authorized government official would brief the press on background when a new proposal or other significant event was planned. Timbie added, however, that some officials were given to "free-lancing"—talking to reporters without authorization to influence what was going on.[5]

Edward Rowny, chief negotiator of strategic arms control

and, later, special adviser to the president for arms control, strongly supported Timbie on this point, condemning the leaking in Washington that plagued INF:

This country leaks like a sieve. The "ship of state" is the only ship that leaks from the top. There was a combination of people waiting to talk, being ill-disciplined and lacking any real sanctions over them. Also, the kind of investigative reporting goal that the press took on for itself meant there were an awful lot of leaks going on in the arms control business—mostly from staffers in various departments, trying to have one-upmanship over the other agencies.[6]

Rowny gave backhanded credit to the press for using its system of gathering and corroborating information between government sources. Reporters evidently learned more than they were supposed to or would have otherwise.

Overall, these interviews show that even though an article or news story might integrate official sources of information, the press could not be characterized as dependent. Those sources often mirrored internal debate over INF policy and frequently offered greater detail than the administration perhaps would have wished.

Officials confirmed that when reporters gathered information from government sources, they would play these sources against one another to get a more complete picture of what was going on. Most officials—Kenneth Adelman notwithstanding—also recognized that the press balanced this information with material from alternative, nongovernment sources. These interviews with officials support the patterns of media information gathering found in the content analysis.

Officials' Views of "How Biased the Press"

According to officials interviewed, the administration did everything possible to affect what was said in the media by focusing its efforts on reiterating and clarifying its policy and position on INF. The Reagan administration, perhaps better than any previous administration, understood the importance of working with and through the press to influence the content of coverage.

Despite these intentions, officials did not seem pleased with how reporters presented the issue. Perceptions among officials of how the press covered INF fall into three broad categories. First, according to officials, the press was too eager for an agreement, willing to compromise anything for arms control. Press bias in favor of an agreement was communicated through the coverage and created a sense of urgency about INF, which, in turn, put pressure on the administration to change policy and on the negotiators to make concessions.

Second, though the press naturally gravitates toward controversy, some officials felt that reporters focused too much on debate within the administration. They also believed press attention to these internal disputes exacerbated the tensions and gave a "sensationalistic" quality to the INF coverage.

Finally, some officials found the coverage focused too much on the "political dimension" of the INF issue. That is, reporters emphasized liberal versus conservative or executive versus Congress angles over what officials considered more weighty— albeit somewhat dry—details of the arms control process.

Eager for Agreement

Kenneth Adelman said the press "hyped," or emphasized, arms control in disproportion to its actual importance. Adelman believed the media created an undue sense of urgency about the negotiations by equating an agreement on INF with peace itself. "In the press at that time [1981 through 1983], arms control was equated with peace. You needed an arms control agreement to have peace."[7]

Richard Perle supported Adelman's view, saying that the coverage reflected a media system eager for the United States to reach an agreement on INF with the Soviets—so eager, Perle went on, that the press often failed to be evenhanded in its reporting. "Because journalists were very keen to see an agreement and were less concerned about the content of the agreement, the press tended to characterize the administration sticking with 'zero' as rigid and inflexible."[8]

Solid support came from Edward Rowny on this point; he found the American press generally impatient and often more critical of U.S. positions than that of the Soviet Union. Rowny noted that although the Reagan administration made a conscious effort to broaden its foreign policy agenda and remove arms control as the centerpiece of that policy, the press never followed suit. "The press had a 'cultural lag' there, believing that arms control was all-important."[9]

Eugene Rostow, director of the Arms Control and Disarmament Agency from 1981 to 1983, was quick to agree that the media was preoccupied with arms control and apparently was prejudiced against the administration. He pointed to the "walk in the woods" affair as a leak that the United States wanted to occur. Rostow believed the episode was so startling to the American media that they "left it alone."

> That's the whole damn thing about leaks and talking to the press. Reporters aren't prepared to hear it. That's the trouble with Talbott's book; he didn't want to believe it either. He couldn't believe that we could do anything right and that the Russians would turn down a compromise. The press was determined that nothing could happen in the nuclear field that wasn't our fault.[10]

According to these officials, the press presented INF in such a way as to emphasize the need for an agreement, even equating an arms control agreement with peace. Further, they believed the media tended to blame the administration if obstacles arose to reaching a compromise with the Soviets.

Public Feuding

The second broad category of official opinion on press coverage was also critical of the media for focusing too much attention on divisions within the administration over policy. Richard Perle believed the press exacerbated these problems "by reporting the outlook of the State Department," which favored compromise with the Soviets and coincided with the arms control bias of the press. Both press opinion and general State Department opinion emphasized flexibility and concessions to reach an agreement. "The press was principally interested in the divisions within the administration, which certainly didn't help. It telegraphed to the Soviets over and over again that if they hung in there and resisted agreeing to the zero option, the American position might change."[11]

Max Kampelman agreed that "reporters were frequently looking for fights between the Departments of State and Defense."[12] Kampelman's predecessor, Paul Nitze, also felt that the press overemphasized differences in the administration. Nitze added philosophically, however, "That's what Washington is interested in—Who loves who? Who hates who?"[13]

Officials noted that the press was naturally attracted to controversy. In arms control, the controversial angles, rather than consensus and agreement, were highlighted. Controversy made for more interesting reading, increasing opportunities for both publication and bigger headlines.

John Woodworth, deputy negotiator on the U.S. INF team, pointed out that the inclination of the press to gravitate toward controversy tended to highlight opposition to administration policy. Media attentiveness to administration critics, to issues such as the nuclear freeze, and to the internal battle over policy was, Woodworth alleged, "not very helpful to the process."[14]

One former administration official qualified this argument, saying that in their coverage, the American media were not necessarily antagonists but rather "gainsayers, second guessers." In this role, the press was after stories that might provoke controversy, rather than reporting issues straightforwardly. "Just read anything that Jeff Smith wrote, and you'll see what I'm talking about."[15]

Jeffrey Smith, reporter for the *Washington Post*, felt that infighting over policy within the administration was an integral part of the INF story. More than other reporters, Smith emphasized interadministration debates. Still, Smith symbolized the general penchant of reporters to focus on contentious aspects of the issue.

The Political Dimension

The general debate over INF policy was not, according to James Timbie, reporters' only angle in approaching the issue. With respect to the final category of official opinion on the tone of press coverage, Timbie said that journalists overemphasized politics, portraying issues or events in such a way that the story would be printed on the front page. Giving the piece a political slant increased the chances that any individual reporter's byline would appear higher up in the day's newshole.

"Fair" is not the first word that comes to mind. . . . Reporters were trying to uncover the "political dimension" of INF—Republican versus Democrat, White House versus the Congress, or State Department versus Defense Department. The press emphasized personality and the political dimension over factual accounts of the negotiations.[16]

Some officials felt political bias extended beyond mere focus on politics. Some saw that bias as partisanship or even ideology. Patrick Glynn, special assistant to the director of ACDA, concluded, "The coverage was partisan, always partisan." By and large, Glynn alleged, the reporters covering INF were one-sided and even made factual errors when writing up the details. Addressing the ideological dimension, he further suggested that a "largely Democratic press" did not make it easy for a Republican administration to get favorable coverage of its policy.

There's certainly a tacit establishment consensus about what does get play in the press and what doesn't; what should be covered and what shouldn't. There was an implicit "party line" in the press corps: there was a cowboy in the White House, and they [the media] had to do something to calm him down and get him back on the ranch with respect to arms control.[17]

Ronald Barteck, an intelligence officer on the arms control intelligence staff and a member of the INF negotiating delegation in Geneva, who also found the press inaccurate on occasion, took a broader view of the political bias in the coverage. "There are always skews in political spectrum of the coverage. There are newspapers that have commentators on the left, and newspapers that have commentators on the right. You've got to expect that."[18]

Eugene Rostow gave an example of how he and chief negotiator Paul Nitze worked out an arrangement with *Time* magazine reporter Strobe Talbott in an effort to head off press bias in the coverage of INF.

At the beginning of the administration, we agreed to keep Strobe Talbott fully briefed off the record. We knew what the previous books had been [full of leaks and inaccuracies]. . . . So, we agreed to do it . . . not to control leaks but to keep him on the straight and narrow path.

Rostow went on to say, however, that this plan had less than satisfactory results. "We didn't succeed at all—not a bit! He wasn't going to listen to anything he didn't want to hear."[19]

The consensus among officials interviewed was that press coverage tended to sensationalize the arms control process. INF officials also believed that press bias was a factor, but a secondary factor, in media coverage. Mainly the bias was toward the dramatic and conflictual, although there was some of both sensationalism and political slant.

Importance and Role of the Press

Evidence presented thus far on the "where" and "how" of news product on INF emphasizes the autonomy of the press—its power to select, characterize, and present the news. The government did not exercise control over the content or context of the coverage. Indeed, officials acknowledged that the administration was often put on the defensive, responding to issues, events, spin, or context that ran counter to official policy or interests.[20]

We must now ask what this autonomy or independence meant for the role of the press in the INF process. Officials were evidently conscious of the importance of the press to both policymaking and negotiating. In the case of INF, public diplomacy played a greater part than with any previous arms control agreement, and certainly the press, and access to the press, were key factors to success. What officials had to say about the role of the press as communicator and as respondent helps in answering this question.

Never Ignore a Reporter

Officials agreed that the press was an important part of their daily operations during INF, and they spent considerable effort on maintaining good relations with that group. Paul Nitze, who headed the delegation in the first round of the negotiations from 1981 through 1983, explained that he made it a point to "take the press seriously." "Journalists have a serious job to do, and they can help you or they can hurt you. The corollary of that is always answer the telephone calls of a press man. Don't ignore him."[21]

Max Kampelman, who served as chief negotiator on INF from 1985 to 1987, made the same point. Kampelman was, if anything, more critical of the press than Nitze.[22] He had published more than one piece before coming to Geneva that was hostile to the prestigious press. The media, he believed, was essential for public understanding, but the press also wielded a great deal of independent power. "I myself can never forget and never ignore the fact that you're dealing with a medium that can cut you up. To that extent, you better be wary and understand it [the press] as a potential adversary. I never forget that."[23]

Kampelman addressed the two roles of the press presented here—those of communicator and of respondent. The media figured into public diplomacy, first, as a means to communicate ideas and increase understanding for the U.S. position. Second, as Kampelman noted, the press might also be considered a "potential adversary." Rather than adversary, per se, that idea is presented in this study as press as respondent.

Lines of Communication

Far and away the most commonly expressed goal among U.S. officials involved in either making policy or negotiating on INF was to "get the message out." The press was absolutely key in this effort, representing the primary medium for communicating policy and opinion.[24]

John Woodworth, who worked both as a representative for the secretary of defense and as a deputy negotiator on the U.S. INF team, understood the importance of communication in creating a base of support. "The strategy was to carve out a comprehensible position with very clear objectives, to make sure those objectives were defensible, to articulate those objectives over and over."[25]

Getting the message out was, evidently, only the first step

in the public diplomacy process. Communicating through the press also served as the instrument for battle in the public relations war with the Soviets. In combination with the private diplomacy going on in Geneva, the idea was to use the media effectively against the Soviets to "win the public debate" because, as John Woodworth said, "All of the Soviet negotiating positions were designed for their impact on public opinion."[26] More than one official said the press had been very important in making sure the Soviets did not "out-public-relations" them.

Ronald Barteck commented that the members of the Soviet negotiating team actively joined this battle for the Western press.

The Soviets tried to capture access to our media. We, along with our NATO allies, were trying to utilize our own media effectively. There were very few substantive interagency meetings in those days that didn't include a very healthy dose of "How do we play this publicly?"[27]

One official even said that the U.S. negotiating team had probably violated the rules established with the Soviets for dealing with the press out of concern for public perceptions.[28] Those rules limited contact between the delegations and the press in an effort to maintain diplomatic confidentiality.

In this public diplomacy, the press operation had two distinct aspects. One was the rather well-structured public relations effort, considered key in the more active stages of the negotiations. This stage was largely a matter of public forum debate, posturing, and trying to win the public debate through the media. Second, during the slower periods, the press was considered vital in exerting pressure on the Soviets in the negotiations.[29]

The appointment of Max Kampelman as chief negotiator during the second round of INF negotiations, 1985 to 1987, was viewed, in part, as a nod to the highly public nature of the process. Officials generally acknowledged that Kampelman operated more publicly than his predecessor and was adept at handling the press. "There was much more willingness in 1985 through 1987 to see the press, mostly in terms of backgrounders. The Soviets were still playing to the public. They had this compulsion, almost, to try out a position and see how it would work in the public."[30] Kampelman used his skill in press relations to gain support in the public, to show he was open to the media, and to let reporters see how "forthcoming" the United States was and how "dogmatic" the Soviets were.

The administration apparently considered the press and press relations to be an important part of its strategy of public diplomacy in INF. The press, however, was also the means through which different parts of the government communicated with one another. According to officials, the *New York Times* and *Washington Post* "defined reality" for the elite community in and around Washington.

By and large, the *Post* and *Times* have far more effect on policymakers than the networks do. Because when you're in the government, you get home too late to watch the evening news. So you end up catching up with the news the following morning. You read your clips . . . those daily news clips go around to everyone in government and everyone in the arms control community. . . . It was the *Times* and *Post* whose clips would get in there. They were the ones that ruled the roost.[31]

Communicating through the press also created problems for the administration. Because of the public nature of INF, people in different parts of the bureaucracy leaked information to the press in an effort to influence the political agenda. "There's obviously a policy battle that's going on, and people all through the arms control process have at various times resorted to leaking to get their way—to try and push the political dimension."[32]

Leaks were the vehicles by which officials used the power and exposure of the press for their own advantage. Very often, these leaks were the result of interagency rivalries.

Ronald Barteck, an intelligence officer on the arms control intelligence staff and a member of the INF negotiating delegation in Geneva, explained that competition for political primacy through the media became commonplace, several departments and agencies entering the fray.

There was a lot of infighting back here . . . any time the OSD [Office of the Secretary of Defense] felt that the White House was not paying enough attention to its position and they had lost the interagency battle over a particular issue, *they would use a press leak to expose the flank of their adversary.* There were times when the OSD would do it. There were times the White House would do it . . . for their own designs. There were even elements in ACDA, the sands were never entirely clean in that regard for the same reason.[33]

Richard Perle agreed with Barteck that Washington was full of "talkative people." Opinions varied, however, on which group was the most talkative. Perle, formerly affiliated with the Department of Defense, felt that the leaks usually originated from the Department of State.[34] The two chief negotiators for INF disagreed about the primary source of Washington leaks. Max Kampelman pointed to congressional staff, but Paul Nitze believed the White House was also involved.[35]

Though senior and junior officials thought it was very difficult to keep anything out of the eye of the press, many people in the administration and bureaucracy were not above using access to the media to advance personal political causes. In a sense, the press was serving as a communicator both on a collective level—to articulate official policy and objectives and to counteract similar efforts by the Soviets—and on an individual level—to advance the personal political objectives of those in official positions.

How Responsive the Press?

In its role as communicator, the press was an important instrument in the public diplomacy maneuvers of both the United States and the Soviet Union. The press itself, according to officials, became a participant in the arms control dialogue. "The Soviets thought they had us trapped, cornered with regard to arms control. They believed that they could keep pushing our public, working our press. I don't think the average American was attuned to the degree to which the press was playing a pressure game."[36]

Data from the content analysis support the notion that the media were, indeed, "playing a pressure game" with the administration. The data are particularly telling for the period between 1981 and 1983. The press was critical of the government's commitment to deployment of INF and appeared strongly biased in favor of reaching an agreement with the Soviets. The administration faced a great deal of opposition to its policies on INF from the press.

In this instance, the press—consciously or unconsciously—was apparently using its position as communicator to lobby in favor of its own pro-arms-control bias. Editorials for the period 1981 through 1987 showed a clear pattern of responsiveness on this issue. That is, when the United States appeared less committed to arms control, the media tended to be more critical. As the United States seemingly became more serious about negotiating, press coverage was less critical. The same pattern was evident in press criticism of the Soviets in the 1984 to 1985 period. After their 1983 walkout of the negotiations, coverage of the Soviet position in the media became more critical.

Press opinion on INF was particularly important because officials acknowledged that they had no way of finding out public opinion about INF with any certainty and relied on the press for their impression of how a particular policy or strategy was received. The American public was not attuned to the INF issue. Thus the press itself was apparently responding to the political agenda.

The effectiveness of the press as respondent was exemplified in the development of the administration's zero option. The media coverage early in 1981 had been highly critical of the U.S. deployment policy. The administration responded with a plan designed, to a significant degree, for its public diplomacy value. The administration had no clear arms control strategy in early 1981. The press responded with a fairly strong critique, and the administration introduced the zero option as a means to relieve this pressure from the media.

The Design of Zero

Publicity and press response were key considerations in the original calculus behind the zero option.

Arms control is 90 percent public relations. It's a public relations exercise. The Reagan administration understood that better than the preceding administration.

Part of the reason you're engaging in arms control negotiations is to maintain a level of public support for your defense policy and your political position. It's a public relations war—it's a propaganda war.[37]

There was a certain mind-set in the Reagan administration behind both the zero option, specifically, and arms control, generally. This mind-set consisted of three different parts. First, the administration was clearly skeptical of previous arms control negotiations, believing that most agreements with the Soviets had not been in the best interests of the United States. Second, despite this belief, the administration recognized the *public* necessity of incorporating some sort of arms control program into its defense strategy. Without some concession to negotiations on nuclear arms, it would have been difficult to rally support for the planned deployment of INF in Europe. Finally, if arms control were to be part of that strategy, it had to be meaningful by creating actual reductions and positive security benefits to the West.

It is important not to underestimate the importance of press relations in this formula and the value of the zero option in this regard.

The Soviets were not at the negotiations to reach an agreement, but to win a public relations battle. We needed something that could make some sense from a security standpoint, but equally and more fundamentally had to be publicly solid, salable, and give *us* the moral high ground.[38]

While the administration was seeking moral high ground, its press coverage was at the bottom of a hole—in 1981, media coverage of INF was highly critical of government policy.

Kenneth Adelman agreed that the widespread coverage given to the antinuclear demonstrations was a consideration in adopting the zero option. "Reagan chose the zero option because it fit into his antinuclear bias. We supported it because it was easy to verify, simple to understand, and it would preempt the peace movement."[39]

Richard Perle, the recognized author of the zero proposal, believed a simple idea that would resonate clearly had advantage over a complicated one. A great advantage of the double zero, in Perle's view, was both its simplicity and that it would be difficult for the press to report badly.[40]

The political weight of "zero" as an acceptable—even ideal—number was not lost on government officials. Zero could be easily verified, represented arms reduction down to an absolute and historic low, and resonated well in the press. Several of the officials interviewed acknowledged that the zero option was put in place as an acceptable safety net so that the administration could dispense with the public burden of arms control and focus on deployment. "The zero option was perceived as a tool of the right wing conservative element of our government to quash any prospect of progress. . . . It was a Richard Perle ploy . . . designed . . . because arms control was not in our interest."[41]

The zero option fulfilled many of the criteria on the administration's arms control checklist, keeping the press at bay and providing a way for the United States to maintain the moral high ground in the negotiations while proceeding with the planned deployment. Paul Nitze also pointed out that even when the negotiations on INF had just started, "we could have lived happily with it [the zero option], if the Russians agreed to it."[42]

The Press: Active, Interpretive, or Passive

These interviews show that government officials devoted a great deal of time and effort during the INF process to public relations. Public relations, though, often took the form of press relations, that is, how to present policy and information in and to the media.

But why did the administration expend this effort on its relationship with the press? Here, I address the issue of press impact and discuss whether and why the media were so important to the government's strategy for INF. Once again, the format for this discussion will be the three models of press behavior—agenda-reflecting, agenda-building, and agenda-setting.

Agenda-Reflecting

Clearly, officials viewed press behavior as more than simply reflective. Indeed, many complained about the difficulty in getting the message out through the press. Reporters would often ignore the administration's message in favor of related but more controversial news items.

Still, before dismissing the possibility of applying the agenda-reflecting model, we must look at whether the press, from an official standpoint, had an impact on the INF process. Only two comments surfaced during the interviews that suggested the press had no impact on the INF negotiations. These comments came from the chief negotiators on INF, Max Kampelman and Paul Nitze. When asked about the impact of the press, Kampelman said, "I can't say a press story ever undercut me in the negotiations." Later in the interview, however, he went into some detail about how the press had done just that.

The media were sure that the INF treaty could not be achieved without giving up Star Wars. So I had to take issue with that, *because when they would say so openly, they were hurting me in my negotiations*—they were leading the Soviets to believe "Ah, they'll give." Whereas, I'd been telling them to put it out of their heads. *I did not welcome this "sideline kibitzing," which I thought was hurting the negotiations.*[43]

Paul Nitze was equally clear when he said, "I didn't feel any particular pressure from the press for faster action or broader results on INF." Richard Perle, however, pointed to Nitze's "walk in the woods" compromise as a direct result of that pressure.

From 1981 to 1983, the press tended to exaggerate the opposition to deployment in Europe, which created some anxiety on the part of the negotiators themselves. . . . I think Paul Nitze would tell you that concern . . . was a major factor in his motivation behind the "walk in the woods." That's probably the clearest example of a result from the pressure of the press.[44]

Although Nitze would not admit to it, most officials and journalists interviewed agreed that Nitze accepted the "walk in the woods" as a result of pressure from media coverage for some movement toward an agreement.

Agenda-Building

In his defense, Nitze differentiated between pressure from the press and pressure from the public, depicting this relationship in terms that fit with the agenda-building model.

In my view, it wasn't the press that had an impact, it was public opinion. That you have to worry about a great deal. The press did have a degree of impact on public opinion—certainly no protest movement can prosper unless it produces a reaction in the press. That's *how* it prospers. So it's the interaction between public opinion and the press, which is a very important interaction.[45]

Eugene Rostow disagreed with Nitze about the impact of public opinion with respect to INF, dismissing it as unimportant.

I think the most important inference you can draw from this experience is like the famous dog in Sherlock Holmes. It didn't bark. Public opinion didn't become a tidal wave as in the case of Vietnam. It didn't impose any restraints on us that I could feel . . . in devising the program or conducting the negotiations.[46]

The term "public opinion" as Rostow meant it can be misconstrued, however. Rostow referred to the swell of *mass* public opinion against Vietnam and lack of a similar outpouring with respect to the INF issue. Nitze qualified his own use of the term, specifying that he referred to *elite* public opinion. Officials generally agreed that the American public, as a whole, was uninterested in the arms control story and the real battle in arms control was a battle among elites. The "elite community" was loosely defined by Patrick Glynn as "about 200 people in and around Washington who were informed on the arms control issue."

Richard Perle agreed that when he considered public opinion, it was this elite public opinion. The press, Perle believed, not only constituted a large percentage of this elite population but also served as its mouthpiece. "The press was more interested in the story than the public was. . . . I think it's fair to say that the press was acting as the voice of elite public opinion."[47]

John Woodworth agreed with Perle on this issue, saying that the press is a core of educated elite that followed arms control as an issue "both out of inclination and occupational capacity." Woodworth admitted that he, too, got his impression of public opinion from the press.[48]

Kenneth Adelman, however, bluntly dismissed public opinion as a factor during the INF process and considered the media to be the real force, particularly in policymaking. Sounding very much like a proponent of the agenda-setting school of media behavior and impact, and in contrast to his comments about press origination, Adelman said, "We react to press coverage, rather than public opinion, because you have no way of finding public opinion. I think it's true that the press . . . is a real player in the policy world."[49]

Although the chief negotiators for INF, Paul Nitze and Max Kampelman, were both reluctant to admit outright that the press influenced the negotiations, they did find that the media occasionally handicapped their capacity to negotiate.

Kampelman was outspoken with regard to his awareness of the power of the press. Nitze, however, believed that it was public opinion, using the press as a venue for expression, that wielded the power. Even Nitze admitted that by public opinion he referred not to mass public opinion but to elite opinion.

The agenda-building model suggests that the press, by providing context and emphasis to particular aspects of the government's agenda or a particular issue, can foster not only public interest and awareness but public action. Nitze apparently agrees with this line of reasoning. Many other officials, however, apparently believe that the press itself became more than a mouthpiece for either the administration or the public. The press was, in this case, the surrogate for public opinion.

If this was indeed so, then the three-way relationship between the government, the press, and public opinion found in the agenda-building model was actually a two-way arrangement. That is, the media were not only providing context and focus to INF but reaction and commentary as well. Overall, the resourceful, aggressive, and adversarial nature of the press, described by a majority of the government officials interviewed, is more in keeping with the agenda-setting model of press behavior.

Agenda-Setting

During these interviews with government officials, the most common theme in response to questions about press behavior and press impact was the consistent bias in the media to pursue arms control and reach an agreement. The notion of arms control as "90 percent public relations" does not appear to be too far from the truth. Administration appointees and career bureaucrats alike focused attentively on how particular policies or positions would play in the press.

Officials agreed that the press was more interested in reaching an agreement than were the American people. Also, in its impact on the government's agenda, Patrick Glynn admitted that press demand was a good part of the reason that the administration even pursued the negotiations and that there was powerful pressure from the media for concessions. "There would have been far less pressure to make unilateral gestures by cutting programs or even entering the negotiations had not the press by 1980 been converted, essentially, into a lobby on behalf of arms control."[50]

The notion of the media as an arms control lobby should be qualified. As Richard Perle stated, press coverage always has some impact but, in the case of INF, it was not necessarily unidirectional. "I think the net effect of the press was different after 1983 than before. It was a source of pressure on us before 1983 and a source of pressure on the Russians after."[51]

This difference is borne out by data from the content analysis, which showed the coverage to be most critical of U.S. policy in the first three years of the period, 1981 through 1983. Although print coverage remained somewhat more critical of the U.S. position than of the Soviet, overall, reporting quantified as neutral vastly predominated coverage in the *Times* and *Post* from 1984 through 1987. Network coverage was more critical of the Soviet Union, with respect to INF, in both 1984 and 1985.

In setting or at least influencing the official agenda, the early years would generally be considered most important. The press, by affecting the official course of action on INF early on, would tend to have both a more profound and a more prolonged impact.

Officials acknowledged that the first years of INF, 1981 to 1983, were, indeed, the most difficult in terms of press coverage. The administration was under tremendous pressure from the press in these three years to reach an agreement at any cost.

Essentially, what the media wanted was an agreement. The press didn't really care what the agreement contained. They didn't really care if we gave anything up—we should make whatever concessions necessary to get an agreement. That was the theme. The press was always pushing it, day in and day out. And if you weren't willing to give things up to get an agreement, you were a bad person and probably wanted nuclear war.[52]

Several administration officials gave credit to the White House for not yielding to the press. The "walk in the woods" proposal was viewed as the only point at which the government wavered in its resolve to do what it felt was best, as opposed to what would sell.

The persistence of the media in trying to push the arms control agenda took on a life and meaning of its own.

To the press, I think it had become arms control as a secular religion at that time. It was really religious. People were dedicated to it, viewed it as a be-all and end-all, thought it held the key to solving the Cold War, thought it held the key to preventing nuclear war.[53]

Arms control was one of the most visible foreign policy activities at that time. Edward Rowny noted that the press seldom felt it was their role to speak for the administration. More often, the media were in an "investigatory mode" and felt their role was to be the opposition. Rowny admitted that in the early days, the press made the negotiating situation "very difficult."

At times the press editorials would call for rapid results, so it would put pressure on us to move faster, make more concessions. Other times, some of the information that was leaked would give the Soviets an argument that would cause them to look into the information, research it, try to find out what was behind it, and then build on it. That slowed things down.[54]

According to government officials, the press was pushing the arms control agenda and putting pressure on the administration for an agreement. Several of the interviewees attributed this to the liberal bias of both the journalistic community and the media establishment that supports and maintains that community.

The way the press presented INF was generally viewed as overly representative of a liberal constituency in favor of arms control. One official went so far as to suggest that certain reporters were assigned to cover INF because of their known bias for arms control.

Both the *New York Times* and *Washington Post* assign reporters to cover arms control who were not reporters but advocates for arms control. Michael Gordon and Jeff Smith, they're both partisans of arms control. I believe it was a deliberate decision on the part of both newspapers because they believed in arms control. This was a "cause," and they knew how to use the guys they'd hired. When you have Smith and Gordon dictating the news, you're going to have a pro-arms-control slant on every story—which by pro-arms-control, I mean pro "make concessions, so we can have an agreement."[55]

Such an extreme view was the exception rather than the rule during these interviews. It does highlight, however, the degree to which administration officials truly felt under fire from the press on the INF issue.

As data from the content analysis suggested, the press was not only active but often even adversarial in its relationship with the government. The media cannot be considered simply a tool for the government to communicate its position or get the message out. The press became a surrogate for public opinion, voicing opinion, concern, and approval regarding official INF policy.

Certainly, government officials involved in the seven-year epic of INF believed that the press played an important role in the process and had substantial impact on the course and conduct of events. James Timbie summed up this view of press behavior with a single phrase: "The press definitely had an impact on the course of the negotiations. These things don't occur in a vacuum, you know."[56]

What may be most telling is that the content data, and even the journalists interviewed for this study, support Timbie. We would expect the negotiators to claim the press was adversarial or even advocative. But a majority of the reporters—who in their professional interest should deny this sort of thing—also felt they had been more active than passive. The press was definitely revealed, by direct test—quantitative evidence—and by interview—qualitative evidence—to do much more than reflect the administration's agenda. The press can be characterized best as agenda-setting in its work, role, and behavior.

CHAPTER 7

Conclusion

The President reigns for four years, but Journalism reigns forever.

—Oscar Wilde

In reviewing the literature on press-government relations, I found contradictions between the different schools of thought and even within them. In retrospect, it becomes clearer why there is so much confusion and contention among those who study the relationship between U.S. policymakers and the media. Even setting aside the ideological dimension of the confusion and contention, neither the content analysis nor the interviews with journalists and officials alone would have been sufficient evidence to make a judgment on this relationship in the case of INF. I hope that this study, based on both of these elements, provides greater clarity.

There were two goals at the outset of the study. The first was to assess the role of the press in the arms control process. The second was to define the relationship between press reporting, government policymaking, and public response in this process.

A theoretical framework of three different models was established to help guide and serve as parameters for the study. Two of the models, agenda-setting and agenda-building, were pre-established theories in the literature on the media. Agenda-setting emphasizes the independence of the press from the government in gathering and presenting information, as well as in influencing the official agenda.

Agenda-building describes the press-government relationship as more interactive and introduces the element of public opinion into the equation. Advocates of the agenda-building model do not believe the media have the power to affect the official agenda, per se, but can affect public discourse on issues by providing context and focus. It is public response, according to this model, that then marshals itself to change government policy.

The third model, agenda-reflecting, though not formally christened in the existing literature, was created for this study. This model represents the views of people writing on press behavior who believe the media are dependent on the government and serve basically as a conduit for information from the government to the public. The press, serving as a transmitter in this theory, does not have the power to affect either policy or the official agenda.

Individual pieces of evidence from the content analysis and interviews might be interpreted in such a way as to support any one of the three theories. But which is best? Here, I will take a last look at all the data, content, and interviews and assess the relevance of each of the models. In contrast to most of the preceding chapters, I will begin with agenda-reflecting, in the end the weakest argument, move then to agenda-building, and finally, to agenda-setting—the best of the models.

Agenda-Reflecting

The case for agenda-reflecting, based on both content and interview data, is the least viable of the three models. The agenda-reflecting theory did not fit the patterns found in the data on the three basic questions asked in the study—where the press got its information, how it presented that information to the public, and what impact this presentation had on official policy.

As for where the press was getting information on INF, both the content analysis of network and print news and interviews with journalists and officials showed that the press was not solely dependent on the government for information. Print and network data from 1981 through 1987 indicated that a consistent and significant percentage of media origination was nongovernment sources.

The interviews with journalists and officials supported this finding. Reporters did not feel that they were dependent on their contacts in the administration and bureaucracy as the only sources of information available. Though official contacts were important, journalists routinely cross-checked or augmented this information with other sources.

In checking information between different government sources, reporters often ran across diverse opinions within the bureaucracy itself. Both journalists and officials admitted that the government failed to present a monolithic point of view on the course of INF policy. This ensured a margin of independence in news coverage because often there was no single, absolute government line.

Of the officials interviewed, only Kenneth Adelman, director of the Arms Control and Disarmament Agency, thought that reporters were dependent on the people in government for information on INF. All of the other government personnel interviewed believed that journalists were in no way dependent and frequently used alternative sources outside of the administration and bureaucracy.

Content and interview data on how the press then presented this information also tend to weaken the case for the agenda-reflecting model. Evidence from the content analysis showed that press coverage of U.S. policy on INF was largely critical of the administration's course, particularly in the first three years, 1981 through 1983. If the media were simply reflecting the government's agenda, the data would have indicated a more passive press.

Government officials confirmed that they had to work hard to get the message out through the press. Officials further complained that even if the message got through, the press did not present it in a way that was favorable to the administration. Eugene Rostow made an attempt to establish a relationship with reporter Strobe Talbott to make sure the official story was told. Talbott, according to Rostow, "wasn't going to listen to anything he didn't want to hear," which, evidently, included the message Rostow was trying to get across.

The question of press impact was addressed through interviews with journalists and officials. Though reluctant to admit to any influence, a majority of the reporters believed that they did have some effect on both INF policy and agenda. Only Michael Gordon asserted that news coverage had no impact, though, when questioned about the coverage of specific events, even Gordon admitted that the press, in covering such issues, could have had an impact.

Most journalists acknowledged that they did have a role in pressuring the administration toward arms control. Officials interviewed agreed with this notion. Chief negotiator Max Kampelman stated that he always viewed the press as a potential adversary that had the power to hurt him in his negotiations.

These impressions of press behavior and impact, along with the data from the content analysis, contradict the agenda-reflecting notion of a passive press transmitting information from the government to the public. Only the pattern of events-ism in the press coverage hinted at a possible reflecting tendency in the media. Eventsism states that the administration's agenda acts as the driving force behind peaks in press coverage.

Though peaks in INF coverage did generally correspond to official events, both the UN session on disarmament and the state referenda on the nuclear freeze stand out as notable, non-government exceptions. For the first three years of the study, nearly one-third of the events representing surges in coverage did not pertain to the official agenda.

Again, too, we must keep in mind how the press reported on U.S. policy with respect to INF. The tenor of the coverage was generally critical of the administration, particularly during the first three years. It is not unusual to find the press covering government events because these events are news. In how they were covered, though, the media were not simply reflecting government policies or agenda.

Overall, both the content data and interviews showed that the press played a more active role in INF than the agenda-reflecting model would allow. The media were not simply transmitting government information or the official line. The agenda-reflecting model does not go far enough toward explaining either press behavior or press impact.

Agenda-Building

The agenda-building model suggests that the press builds on the official agenda by providing context and framework to issues from that agenda. The media are able to do this through the use of alternative sources of information, as well as by adjusting the focus of the coverage.

A key component of the agenda-building model is that the press itself does not have the power to alter policy. Public opinion, based on information from the media, serves as the agent of change in influencing government policy. The power of the press is in its ability to shape public perceptions through the information, context, and focus it provides.

Both content and interview data as to where the press was getting information on INF could support the agenda-building model, which allows for a mix of both government and nongovernment sources. Particularly in the early years, 1981 through 1983, nongovernment sources were the most active—in the form of protests and demonstrations—and thus alternative sourcing was readily available to and frequently used by the media.

These nongovernment sources also could have influenced how the press was approaching and presenting the INF issue. The media might be viewed as building on the administration's agenda by integrating the alternative content provided by these sources. That content offered opinions and focus to the issues that were not necessarily consistent with those of the government.

This notion is supported by the criticism of U.S. policy in early years, when nongovernment organizations were most active in favor of arms control and alternative sources were more available to the press. The negative coverage tapered off in the later years of the period, when the administration appeared more committed to pursuing arms control and the activity of nongovernment organizations dropped off.

These data suggest the agenda-building model because it appears the press was not establishing the arms control agenda, per se, but building on or augmenting it when the information was available. The media were able to emphasize priorities and focus on issues that did not always top the official agenda. This behavior is consistent with the interactive role assigned to the press by the agenda-building model.

But what did the interviews tell us about the third dimension—media impact? Public opinion is an important facet of the agenda-building model. According to this theory, it is not the press but public opinion that affects policy. Public opinion is shaped by media coverage.

Officials who were closely involved with INF policy and the negotiations were in the best position to assess whether public opinion—or the press—had an impact on their operation. Only Paul Nitze believed that public opinion had an impact and that the press played a role because of its interaction with public opinion. He went on to qualify, however, that he was actually referring to elite public opinion.

All of the other officials interviewed agreed that the media were much more interested and attuned to the INF issue than the public. Kenneth Adelman acknowledged that officials react to press coverage, rather than public opinion, because they have no way of determining public opinion. Rostow likened the lack of public outcry to the famous dog in Sherlock Holmes; neither the dog nor public opinion, in this case, barked. Public opinion imposed no restraints and had no impact on either policy or the negotiations, according to Rostow. Only a swell of mass public opinion similar to that during the Vietnam War, he continued, would have the visibility to affect policy.[1]

Though the content analysis showed some support for the agenda-building model, the nonrole of public opinion suggests that interaction between press and public was limited, at best. Also, by the end of December 1987, fully 72 percent of Americans in an ABC-Washington Post poll knew little or nothing about the INF Treaty.[2] Though a majority of the public favors arms control, writ large, the mass public was not attuned to the INF issue. On the whole, the agenda-building notion of the press interacting with the public is not supported either by the interviews with officials involved or by these percentages on public awareness.[3]

Agenda-Setting

The apparent lack of press interaction with the public on INF leads us from the agenda-building model to the agenda-setting model of press behavior. Rather than an interactive press, agenda-setting suggests an independent model of press behavior—independent both in the origin of information and the political issues and agenda the press pursues. This independence gives the press the power to influence the political agenda.

As for where the press was getting information on INF, both the content analysis and interviews showed that the press used government and nongovernment sources. Use of nongovernment sources by the *Times* and *Post* surpassed or equaled use of government sources in six of seven years of the study (1981 through 1986).

Interviews with journalists and officials supported these findings and also revealed a system used by reporters when gathering information from sources in government. Reporters commonly cross-checked pieces of information from a source in one agency with sources from other departments. The corroboration or denial reduced a reporter's susceptibility to manipulation from a single source. Journalists agreed that this investigative work was more characteristic of the print media than television because of time restrictions and desire for visuals in network reporting.

Data on the tone of INF coverage, both from the interviews and the content analysis, indicated that the press was critical of U.S. policy, particularly from 1981 through 1983. This pattern of criticism tends to refute the notion of government manipulation or control of the news process. That is, even when reporters integrated government sources into their articles, data on how that information was presented indicated independent, agenda-setting press behavior.

The timing of press coverage inherently critical of administration policy on INF also suggested media independence and hinted at influence. The press was most negative in its reporting during the first three years, 1981 through 1983. These early years in the life of an issue are, according to the agenda-setting model, most important in affecting government policy.

The *Times* and *Post* were highly critical of U.S. policy in 1981, during the debate in NATO over the deployment of INF in Western Europe, and, largely, before President Reagan announced the zero option. Negative coverage continued to run high over the next two years, 1982 and 1983, and often focused on issues or organizations outside the government or the government's control.

This negative press coverage came while the Reagan administration appeared most committed to deployment and less concerned about arms control negotiations—the zero option notwithstanding. Data on how information on INF was presented point to an independent press—a press that was attempting to drive the political agenda in the direction of arms control.

Officials said that this atmosphere often put them on the defense vis-à-vis the media and that trying to defuse criticism from the press became part of their daily routine. Patrick Glynn remarked, "You're obviously trying to get your point across, but you were usually responding to criticism from the press. . . . There was a huge avalanche of criticism [about INF], and we had to dig out."[4]

Data from the second part of the study, the combination of interviews from reporters and officials, allow for some speculation about the impact of the media on the INF process and how that impact related to the three models. Though uncomfortable with questions regarding their own role and impact, reporters provided some important insights, even a few revelations.

According to data from the interviews, an agenda-setting model appears best to describe press behavior. From what was said by both journalists and officials, the press played two important roles that very likely influenced both perceptions and policy in the case of INF. First, the press served as a communicator of information between different groups either interested or directly involved in arms control. Second, the press was apparently an important player in its own right as a respondent to information and policy.

As a communicator, the press was a source for people and organizations outside of the bureaucratic structure—the attuned public—to see and understand what people in government were doing. The mass public, though broadly in favor of arms control writ large, was not attuned to the INF issue per se. According to officials, it was the elite public, consisting generally of people in and around Washington, that was attentive to the specifics of arms control policy and process.

The media were also routinely used during INF as a means of communication for people within government—both interdepartmental and interbranch. The press served as a forum for policy debates between the Departments of State and Defense, as well as between Congress and the executive. Journalists stated that the diversity of opinion on INF within the administration became a major part of the story line.

Although officials believed the press overemphasized these differences, they admitted to relying consistently on the *Washington Post* and *New York Times* for information about what was going on both in and out of the bureaucracy. As Patrick Glynn explained, "The reality in Washington every morning is the *Washington Post*. It arrives at your door and defines your reality."[5]

Particularly in the early years of the study, 1981 through 1983, news coverage was defining government policy in fairly unfavorable terms. Content data and interviews suggest the media were in favor of a stronger commitment to arms control and tried to encourage government policy in that direction.

The power of the press to define reality for policymakers supports an influential, agenda-setting model of behavior. As the content analysis showed, the media were independent both in gathering information and in setting the tone for INF. Combined with the power of the press as communicator to define, according to officials, the political reality of arms control suggests at least an influential, if not an agenda-setting role.

The second part of the media's role in INF is termed here as that of respondent. Quantitative data from the content analysis and qualitative evidence from the interviews suggest that press opinion became a surrogate for public opinion. Awareness of INF among the mass public stood at only 28 percent, even in 1987, when the treaty was signed.[6]

The press itself, according to one reporter, represented a core of educated elite that followed arms control out of interest and not simply occupational necessity. Interviews with both journalists and officials suggested that interest generally stemmed also from a pro-arms-control bias in the media establishment. Data from the content analysis support this idea, indicating that news coverage was most critical of U.S. policy on INF from 1981 through 1983, when the administration appeared least committed to arms limitation.

With respect to the idea of press opinion standing in for public opinion, several officials admitted that they had no way to assess the public's views on INF and relied on the press for a "read" on the public mind. If the media were responding to issues, as well as communicating them, a pro-arms-control bias would have an impact on those perceptions and, hence, political "reality." That is, news coverage generated by a medium with a predisposition in favor of arms control might give an impression that this viewpoint actually carried broader, mass support.

In contrast to the agenda-building model, which points to public opinion as the agent of change in policy, the notion of press as respondent suggests an agenda-setting model of press behavior. It is possible, given the quantitative (content analysis) and qualitative (interview) evidence, that the press, and press opinion, had the power to influence both official policy and the political agenda. A corollary for the agenda-setting model seems appropriate. The press does not tell the public what to think about, but it does tell the government what it should think about.

Officials were certainly aware of the power of the press to shape issues and universally believed the press did have an impact. Perhaps the clearest example of press influence was the zero option. Richard Perle, architect of the proposal, acknowledged that it was invented primarily to offset criticism in the press about the administration's INF deployment strategy in 1981. The proposal, according to Perle, was designed for its value as a public relations tool to help defuse that criticism.

If this was indeed the case, what better evidence of press impact—and the agenda-setting power of the press—than a policy designed specifically for its effect on and consumption by the media? According to officials, the administration was able to hold to the zero option first because of the extensive public-press relations effort surrounding it. Second, the proposal was tailored for its potential for positive play in the media.

The pressure on the administration from the press for some movement in arms control, particularly during 1981 and continuing for the next two years, is consistent with the revised agenda-setting model of press behavior—that the press actually tells the government, not the public, what to think about. Richard Perle and other involved officials stated that this pressure did have an impact both on policy and on the negotiations.

In regard to the "impact" question, officials handling press relations on a daily basis during INF—and the questions of the reporters—acknowledged some press influence with respect to INF. Of the three models—agenda-setting, agenda-building, and agenda-reflecting—the strongest case can be made for agenda-setting. Data from the content analysis on where the press was getting information and how it presented that information to the public support this model of press behavior.

Career bureaucrats and administration appointees alike made it clear that press opinion and press coverage were consistently taken into account in the policymaking and negotiations of INF. It is this qualitative evidence suggesting media influence, along with the quantitative support from the content analysis, that strengthens a conclusion in favor of a modified agenda-setting model of press behavior.

In the end, a new corollary to the existing agenda-setting theory of press behavior was discovered. Bernard Cohen, generally considered the founder of the agenda-setting school of thought, said that although the press does not tell people what to think, "it is stunningly successful in telling its readers what to think about."[7] This study discovered that in the case of arms control, the media were stunningly successful in telling the government what to think about.

Final Remarks

The relationship between press reporting, government policymaking, and public response is by no means a fixed quantity. The issue involved, how it is presented, and official reaction all contribute to both the relationship and the eventual outcome. In the case presented here on INF, it appears that press-government-public interaction can more accurately be described as a bilateral press-government relationship.

Lack of public involvement is neither new nor surprising. Scholars have found that although public opinion might establish general parameters for official policy and action in foreign affairs, these limits tend to be broad and elastic.[8] A majority of Americans are uninterested in U.S. relations with other countries; few keep informed on news of foreign nations.[9]

In accordance with this notion, arms control and INF did not have the potency to mobilize mass public opinion in any meaningful way. Officials involved with INF confirmed that the mass public did not play a role in either policymaking or the negotiations. In an interview with ABC News, Max Kampelman discussed the various sources of pressure on him as an American negotiator. Public opinion was conspicuously absent from Kampelman's list, but the press figured prominently. "The Soviets negotiate on an assumption that an American negotiator is under pressure from the press, from the Congress, from the opposing political party, from the Allies, and may therefore make concessions as a result of those outside pressures."[10]

A study by Doris Graber supports this impression using an example keyed to INF. Immediately before the signing of the treaty, NBC News broadcast an hour-long interview with Soviet leader Mikhail Gorbachev during prime time. Only 15 percent of the national audience tuned in, and of the viewers who regularly watch NBC during that time slot, half changed to other networks.[11]

The relationship, in this case, changed from a three-way press-government-public framework to a bilateral press-government exchange. Officials stated that what they watched and gauged closely was the press, press coverage, and press perceptions. The idea of press as respondent embodies the more active role suggested by the evidence found in this study and corresponds to the proposal made by some academics that the media are public opinion, with respect to foreign affairs.[12]

The corollary to the agenda-setting model warrants repeating. It was the press, particularly in its role as respondent, that told the administration what to think about on the INF issue.

The success of the Reagan administration in INF could be attributed to the fact that officials listened to and understood the power of the media on arms control and INF from the outset. The zero option was, evidently, developed with this in mind and with the understanding that the predominant view in the press—acknowledged by some journalists and supported by data from the content analysis—favored arms control. The administration recognized the media's ability to "encourage" policy in the direction of "appropriate" preferences[13]—in this case, arms control—and developed policy accordingly.

The media have been termed by some scholars the "fourth estate" or fourth branch of government. With regard to the INF negotiations this was the case. The press brought the issue closer to home, yet the mass public proved itself not to be at home. The government was at home—but with the press as invited guest. And the guest—the American news media—clearly made the host consider its wants and needs.

Reference Matter

Notes

Chapter 1

The chapter epigraphs are from interviews with Patrick Glynn, special assistant to director of ACDA, Oct. 18, 1990, and Max Kampelman, chief negotiator on INF, July 26, 1990.

1. Intermediate-range nuclear forces included U.S. and Soviet ground-launched ballistic missiles with a range between 600 and 3,000 miles. For the Soviet Union, these missiles were the SS-4, SS-5, and SS-20. U.S. intermediate-range forces included the Pershing II and the BGM-109G.

2. Talbott, pp. 79–80, discusses European and American reaction to the proposal.

3. Under this compromise, the Soviet Union retained 75 SS-20s; the United States kept 75 ground-launched cruise missile launchers; each side would reduce its nuclear-capable aircraft in Europe to 150; the Soviet Union would freeze its SS20s in the Far East at 90 missiles as well as freeze its SS-21s, SS22s, and SS23s; and the United States would not deploy Pershing IIs.

Chapter 2

1. Cohen, *The Press*, p. 13.

2. See McCombs and Shaw, "The Agenda-Setting Function of the Mass Media"; Weaver et al.; Iyengar, Peters, and Kinder.

3. McCombs and Shaw, "The Agenda-Setting Function of the Press," p. 65.

4. Ranney, pp. 73–74.

5. Linsky, p. 109.

6. Cutler; see also Ledeen.

7. Lang and Lang, p. 61; emphasis added.

8. Ibid., p. 58.

9. Kernell, p. 3.

10. Ibid., p. 162.

11. Lang and Lang, p. 61.

12. Ibid., p. 58.

13. Some sociologists refer to this notion as "hegemony theory," though hegemonists invariably view agenda-reflection as the by-product of capitalist values and practices. For additional information see Gitlin.

14. Sigal, p. 104.

15. Geylin, p. 19.

16. Rosen, *Democracy Overwhelmed*, p. 4.

17. Hess, *The Government/Press Connection*, pp. 110–11.

18. Cutler, p. 113.

19. Becker, p. 364.

20. Hess, *Washington Reporters*; Geylin; Rosen, *Democracy Overwhelmed*.

21. Linsky, p. 13.

22. Ibid., p. 118; emphasis added.

23. Massing, p. 4.

24. Ibid., p. 4.

25. Krepon, "Arms Control Play-by-Play."

26. Kampelman, "Congress, the Media, and the President," p. 90.

27. Ibid., p. 91.

28. Further discussion of this and interviews with other journalists and officials involved in INF appears in subsequent chapters of this book.

Chapter 3

1. Bower, p. 99.

2. A chart on overall amount of coverage is presented later in this chapter. This chart includes data from all three networks, information readily available from the *Vanderbilt Television News Archives Index*.

3. A separate study could be conducted on press coverage of the INF Treaty ratification and how this issue was used in the 1988 presidential election campaign.

4. Adams, "Visual Analysis," in Adams and Schreibman, pp. 155–78.

5. Katz, Adona, and Parness.

6. Robinson and Sheehan, p. 27: "We still think that not including visuals in our study is defensible, because we wanted to use common denominators in our comparisons of television and print. The common denominators are the story and the sentence; so stories and sentences become the more legitimate comparison."

7. "Pronunciamento," in this case, refers to the pronouncements or

statements of government officials. These statements, speeches, or comments can come from either identified or unidentified sources.

8. Government-controlled sources in this chart consist of news leak, identified U.S. government pronunciamento, and unidentified U.S. government pronunciamento. The non-government-controlled group was made up of Soviet pronunciamento, nongovernment pronunciamento, multiple sources, and investigative variables.

9. They were alliance problems, European pressure to negotiate, U.S. domestic pressure to negotiate, and Soviet pressure to negotiate.

10. Data presented seem to support these ideas, as do personal interviews with both former administration officials and journalists in Chapters 5 and 6.

11. Categories that qualify as pro-arms-control include the European antinuclear protest movement, the nuclear freeze movement, European pressure to negotiate on INF, and U.S. domestic pressure to negotiate on INF.

12. The calculations are rather straightforward: 40 percent of the news stories originated from nongovernment sources; 90 percent of that number supported the nuclear freeze, European protests, or an immediate agreement. This 90 percent, in turn, represents 36 percent of all the stories from that year.

13. Personal interviews with both former administration officials and journalists strongly suggest that the zero option was put forward to assuage the debate over INF deployment.

14. Lang and Lang, p. 60.

15. As noted in the preceding case models, 1982 often stands out as a unique year for network coverage of INF. In this year, nongovernment sources dominated network stories, mainly resulting from the popularity of the nuclear freeze movement as an INF-related issue. This year was an isolated case, though, and identified U.S. government pronunciamentos still represented nearly 20 percent of the origination for network stories.

16. This point will be discussed further in Chapters 5 and 6.

Chapter 4

1. Robinson and Clancey, "King of the Hill." See also Robinson and Clancey, "A 98-Pound Weakling?"

2. Only articles from the *Times* were used in this tier of the analysis. The *New York Times* is considered the newspaper of record for international affairs and was selected for that reason.

3. To reduce error and ensure more even distribution, a stratification

method was used to choose the articles. Rather than randomly select the 10 percent or 480 of the 4,800 articles, the sample was stratified first by year and then by month. Reducing the primary sampling unit to a month reduced the sampling error. This way, the data would not be clustered in a single year, yet random selection was preserved.

4. This does not include commentary or editorial variables because these types are based, for the most part, solely on the opinion of the author.

5. In these initial years, the administration's policy was firmly committed to the deployment of medium-range nuclear weapons in Western Europe. As we will see later, a large percentage of the press coverage during these years was critical of official U.S. policy. From 1981 through 1983, the New York Times was actively pursuing aspects of the INF issue, independent of and not particularly helpful to the administration's selected roster.

6. European protests and the freeze movement include articles protesting the deployment of U.S. missiles in Europe, protesting the U.S. military presence in Europe generally, or calling for a freeze on the production and deployment of nuclear weapons.

7. The strong show of support in 1983 could be attributed in part to "damage control" by the Reagan administration. The first-phase deployment of INF in Western Europe was scheduled for November 1983; 1984 was an important presidential election year. The need for a show of strength and foreign policy resolve could not have been lost on the Reagan administration.

8. Individual topics in the New York Times can be grouped according to degree of support or criticism for U.S. policy on INF. Themes generally reflecting positively on U.S. policies are supportive of U.S. policies, Western criticism of Soviet Union, criticism of the European protest movement, and criticism of the U.S. freeze movement. Those themes considered to reflect negatively on U.S. policy were criticism of U.S. policy, Soviet criticism of the West, supportive of the European protest movement, and supportive of the U.S. freeze movement.

9. Figure 23 refers only to data from the New York Times. Unless otherwise noted in this section, figures present data from both the Times and the Post.

10. The only two peaks in coverage of INF during 1982 were the UN session on disarmament and the state votes for referenda supporting a nuclear freeze.

11. This section looks at the sample of 480 news pieces appearing in the Post and Times between 1981 and 1987.

12. Corresponding percentages are as follows: 42 percent critical

versus 22 percent supportive in 1981; 35 percent critical versus 26 percent supportive in 1982; and 34 percent critical versus 28 percent supportive in 1983.

13. Walker, p. 435.

Chapter 5

1. Some of the journalists interviewed for this study requested that their names be withheld from direct attribution.

2. Jeffrey Smith, int., Oct. 26, 1990.

3. Jeffrey Smith, int., Oct. 29, 1990.

4. David Martin, int., Oct. 25, 1990.

5. David Ensor of ABC pointed out that by talking to people who were not part of the government, he was able to get different sides of the issue. He went on to say that the Soviets, in particular, became "more and more important in providing that kind of balance" (int., Dec. 5, 1990).

6. For additional information on the conventional use of backgrounders see Sandman, Rubin, and Sachman, pp. 416–18.

7. Walter Pincus, int., Nov. 1, 1990.

8. Reporter asked to remain anonymous.

9. William Beecher, int., Oct. 29, 1990.

10. David Martin of CBS believed that dealing with government sources in the venue of television makes a reporter susceptible to manipulation. When officials are interviewed, they are on camera, and, as Martin pointed out, "you're stuck with it" and often "duty bound to use it" (int., Oct. 25, 1990).

11. Press bias will also be discussed in Chapter 6. Government officials universally believed that the press was strongly biased in favor of arms control.

12. Reporter asked to remain anonymous.

13. For additional information on press ideology and bias, see Dye, Zeigler, and Lichter, pp. 100–103; Lichter and Rothman; Lichter, Lichter, and Rothman.

14. Reporter asked to remain anonymous.

15. Walter Pincus characterized double zero as "really rather a clever move," proposed because the Europeans demanded that the United States have a position, "not because they [the administration] thought it would get us anywhere" (int., Nov. 1, 1990).

16. Saturation coverage of the antinuclear demonstrations in Europe and the freeze movement in the United States contributed to this negative impression of the administration's strategy for INF. This was, per-

haps, one of the few instances in which television actually played a substantive, even influential role. Protests and demonstrations provided
heady visuals for the electronic media. The content analysis confirmed
that television coverage was most critical in 1981 and 1983. More will
be said about the differences between print and television later.

17. David Martin, int., Oct. 25, 1990.

18. Sigal, pp. 185–86.

19. David Martin, int., Oct. 25, 1990.

20. Walter Pincus, int., Nov. 1, 1990.

21. Jeffrey Smith, int., Oct. 29, 1990.

22. ABC–Washington Post Poll, as reported on *ABC Nightly News*,
Dec. 3, 1987.

23. David Ensor, int., Dec. 5, 1990.

24. Hinckley, p. 70. Hinckley summarizes his discussion about public awareness of INF, saying, "A probable conclusion from these results
is that nearly three of every four Americans are ignorant about basic arms control positions of the two superpowers. . . . [Americans]
are . . . generally ignorant of even the most basic arms control proposals and the specific points of treaties such as the INF accord."

25. Kegley and Wittkopf, p. 309.

26. This evidence will be presented in the following chapter.

27. Walter Pincus, int., Nov. 1, 1990.

28. Ibid.

29. Anonymous journalist.

30. David Ensor, int., Dec. 5, 1990.

31. Ibid.

32. According to journalist Walter Pincus, "Usually the networks
take their lead from . . . the *Times* and *Post*. Arms control was not a
great story for them. For them, arms control was demonstrations. So, if
anything, they skew coverage to demonstrations, rather than the details of what's going on" (int., Nov. 1, 1990).

33. Talbott, p. 118, also talks about how the Soviets attempted to
use this press leak, exploiting "speculation among Americans that the
U.S., by making an offer and then withdrawing it, had doomed any
chance" that the "walk in the woods" package would break the impasse
in the INF negotiations.

34. Anonymous journalist.

Chapter 6

The chapter epigraph is from John Woodworth, int., Oct. 31, 1990.

1. James Timbie, int., Oct. 16, 1990.

2. Richard Perle, int., Feb. 27, 1991.

3. Max Kampelman, int., July 26, 1990.

4. Kampelman went on at some length about his views on leaks. "I never leaked that way—I might leak deliberately in Geneva, if you want to call what I did leaking; really, it wasn't leaking . . . I was not a leaker. I didn't like it, and, frankly, developed nothing but disdain for those in our government who did leak" (int., July 26, 1990).

5. James Timbie, int., Oct. 16, 1990.

6. Edward Rowny, int., Nov. 1, 1990.

7. Kenneth Adelman, int., Oct. 29, 1990.

8. Richard Perle, int., Feb. 27, 1991.

9. Edward Rowny, int., Nov. 1, 1990.

10. Eugene Rostow, int., Oct. 15, 1990.

11. Richard Perle, int., Feb. 27, 1991.

12. Max Kampelman, int., July 26, 1990.

13. Paul Nitze, int., Nov. 13, 1990.

14. John Woodworth, int., Oct. 31, 1990.

15. The official asked to remain anonymous.

16. James Timbie, int., Oct. 16, 1990.

17. Patrick Glynn, int., Oct. 18, 1990.

18. Ronald Barteck, int., Oct. 31, 1990.

19. Eugene Rostow, int., Oct. 15, 1990.

20. Patrick Glynn, int., Oct. 18, 1990.

21. Paul Nitze, int., Nov. 13, 1990.

22. Kampelman, "Congress, the Media, and the President," p. 90.

23. Max Kampelman, int., July 26, 1990.

24. Ronald Barteck, int., Oct. 31, 1990.

25. John Woodworth, int., Oct. 31, 1990.

26. Ibid.

27. Ronald Barteck, int., Oct. 31, 1990.

28. The official asked that this remark not be attributed to him.

29. Ronald Barteck, int., Oct. 31, 1990.

30. John Woodworth, int., Oct. 31, 1990.

31. Patrick Glynn, int., Oct. 18, 1990.

32. Ibid.

33. Ronald Barteck, int., Oct. 31, 1990.

34. Richard Perle, int., Feb. 27, 1991.

35. Max Kampelman, int., July 26, 1990; Paul Nitze, int., Nov. 13, 1990.

36. Patrick Glynn, int., Oct. 18, 1990.

37. Ibid.

38. John Woodworth, int., Oct. 31, 1990.

39. Kenneth Adelman, int., Oct. 29, 1990.
40. Richard Perle, int., Feb. 27, 1991.
41. Ronald Barteck, int., Oct. 31, 1990.
42. Paul Nitze, int., Nov. 13, 1990.
43. Max Kampelman, int., July 26, 1990.
44. Richard Perle, int., Feb. 27, 1991.
45. Paul Nitze, int., Nov. 13, 1990.
46. Eugene Rostow, int., Oct. 15, 1990.
47. Richard Perle, int., Feb. 27, 1991.
48. John Woodworth, int., Oct. 31, 1990.
49. Kenneth Adelman, int., Oct. 29, 1990.
50. Patrick Glynn, int., Oct. 18, 1990.
51. Richard Perle, int., Feb. 27, 1991.
52. Patrick Glynn, int., Oct. 18, 1990.
53. Ibid.
54. Edward Rowny, int., Nov. 1, 1990.
55. The official asked to remain anonymous.
56. James Timbie, int., Oct. 16, 1990.

Chapter 7

1. Richard Perle stated that the administration was more concerned about European public opinion during the early years, 1981–83, because of its potential impact on the INF deployment schedule (int., Feb. 27, 1991).

2. ABC–Washington Post Poll, as reported on *ABC Nightly News,* Dec. 3, 1987.

3. Academics who study the impact of public opinion on foreign policy have found that most Americans are poorly informed and uninterested in complex issues like arms control and tend to go along with most government decisions in this area. For example, Kegley and Wittkopf, p. 299, admit that for most foreign policy decisions, "public opinion provides neither a clear nor a consistent guide to policy making. . . . As a consequence, elites often define their appropriate role as one of leading [public opinion] rather than following."

4. Patrick Glynn, int., Oct. 18, 1990.

5. Ibid.

6. ABC–Washington Post Poll, as reported on *ABC Nightly News,* Dec. 3, 1987.

7. Cohen, *The Press,* p. 13.

8. Almond; Caspary; Nincic, pp. 57–78; Kegley and Wittkopf, pp. 279–84.

9. Reilly, p. 8; Graber; Ornstein, Kohut, and McCarthy.

10. Max Kampelman, interview with ABC News, Dec. 11, 1987. Kampelman seems to believe everybody except the public is involved.

11. As quoted in Dye, Zeigler, and Lichter, p. 328.

12. Kegley and Wittkopf, p. 309.

13. Hinckley, pp. 242–57.

Bibliography

Primary Sources

A. Government Officials

The position(s) of each interviewee during the negotiating period 1980–87 is indicated. The date of the interview(s) is given for each name.

Adelman, Kenneth. Director of the Arms Control and Disarmament Agency (ACDA), U.S. Department of State, 1983–87. Oct. 29, 1990.

Alessi, Victor. Chief of Strategic Affairs Division, Arms Control and Disarmament Agency (ACDA), U.S. Department of State. Oct. 16, 1990.

Barteck, Ronald. Intelligence Officer, Central Intelligence Agency, Arms Control Intelligence Staff, 1984. Political-Military Officer, Political-Military Bureau, Department of State, 1985–87; Member of the Geneva INF Delegation, 1987. Oct. 31, 1990.

Clyne, Norman. Executive Secretary of the U.S. Arms Control Delegation to Geneva. Oct. 24, 1990.

Glynn, Patrick. Special Assistant to Director of Arms Control and Disarmament Agency (ACDA), U.S. Department of State. Oct. 18, 1990.

Kampelman, Max. Chief Negotiator for the INF Talks, 1985–87. July 26, 1990.

Kraemer, Sven. Director of Arms Control, National Security Council (NSC), Defense Policy Staff. Oct. 25, 1990.

Nitze, Paul. Chief of Geneva Arms Control Negotiating Team, 1981–83. Nov. 13, 1990.

Perle, Richard. Assistant Secretary of Defense for International Security Policy (ISP), U.S. Department of State. Feb. 27, 1991.

Rostow, Eugene. Director of the United States Arms Control and Dis-

armament Agency (ACDA), U.S. Department of State, 1981–83. Oct.
15, 1990.

Rowny, Edward. Chief Negotiator for Strategic Arms Reduction Talks,
1981–83; Special Adviser to the President for Arms Control, 1985–
87. Nov. 1, 1990.

Timbie, James. Technical Adviser to the INF Negotiating Team and
Technical Expert for the Arms Control and Disarmament Agency,
U.S. Department of State. Oct. 16, 1990.

Woodworth, John. Staff Member of Arms Control and Disarmament
Agency, U.S. Department of State. Oct. 31, 1990.

B. Reporters

The position(s) of each interviewee during the negotiating period
1980–87 is indicated. The date of the interview(s) is given for each
name:

Beecher, William. *Boston Globe*, Defense and Foreign Affairs Correspondent. Oct. 29, 1990.

Ensor, David. ABC News, State Department Correspondent. Dec. 5,
1990.

Francis, Fred. NBC News, Pentagon Correspondent. Oct. 23, 1990.

Gordon, Michael. *New York Times*, Defense Correspondent. Oct. 22
and 31, 1990.

Martin, David. CBS News, Pentagon Correspondent. Oct. 25, 1990.

Pincus, Walter. *Washington Post*, Congressional Correspondent. Nov.
1, 1990.

Smith, Jeffrey. *Washington Post*, Defense Correspondent. Oct. 26 and
29, 1990.

Talbott, Strobe. *Time* Magazine, Editor. Oct. 24, 1990.

Zelnick, Robert. ABC News, Pentagon Correspondent. Dec. 5, 1990.

Secondary Sources

Adams, William C., and Fay Schreibman, eds. *Television Network
News: Issues in Content Research.* Washington D.C.: George Washington University Press, 1978.

Adelman, Kenneth. *The Great Universal Embrace: Arms Summitry—
A Skeptic's Account.* New York: Simon and Schuster, 1989.

——. "Kenneth Adelman on the Press: 'Terrific,' 'Outrageous,' 'Un-
fair.'" Interview by David M. Rubin and Lee Feinstein. *Deadline*,
Mar.–Apr. 1988, 3–6.

Almond, Gabriel. *The American People and Foreign Policy.* New York:
Praeger, 1960.

Altheide, David L. "Media Hegemony: A Failure of a Perspective." *Public Opinion Quarterly* 48 (1984): 476–90.

Arkin, William M. "New INF Numbers Cast Doubt on Standard Press Tallies." *Deadline*, May–June 1988, 1–2.

Aronson, James. *The Press and the Cold War*. Boston: Beacon Press, 1973.

Becker, Lee B. "Foreign Policy and Press Performance." *Journalism Quarterly* 54 (1977): 364–68.

Bethell, Thomas. "The Myth of an Adversary Press." *Harper's*, Jan. 1977, 33–40.

Binnendijk, Hans, ed. *National Negotiating Styles*. Washington, D.C.: Department of State Publication, Foreign Service Institute, Center for the Study of Foreign Affairs, 1987.

Bobrow, Davis B. "Communication and Information Dimensions of Arms Control: Arms Control Through Communication and Information Regimes." *Political Studies* 8 (1979): 60–66.

Bonafede, Dom. "Geneva Summit Shows How Diplomacy Has Entered the Communications Age." *National Journal*, Dec. 14, 1985, 2861–64.

Bower, Robert T. *Television and the Public*. New York: Holt, Rinehart and Winston, 1973.

Braley, Russ. *Bad News: The Foreign Policy of the New York Times*. 2d ed. New York: Regnery Gateway, 1984.

Bram, Stephen. "What Reporters Think About Arms Control." *Deadline*, Nov.–Dec. 1987, 1–2; Jan.–Feb. 1988, 8–9.

Buchanan, Patrick J. "The Dangers of Television Diplomacy." *TV Guide*, Jan. 28, 1978, A5–A6.

Bullion, Stuart James. "Press Roles in Foreign Policy Reporting." *Gazette* 32 (1983): 179–88.

Caspary, William R. "The 'Mood Theory': A Study of Public Opinion and Foreign Policy." *American Political Science Review* 64 (1970): 536–47.

Center for Law and National Security. "Conference Report on U.S. Military Operations and the Press." *Political Communication and Persuasion* 3 (1985): 69–93.

Chittick, William O. "State Department–Press Antagonism: Opinion Versus Policy-Making Needs?" *Journal of Politics* 31 (1969): 756–71.

Clotfelter, James. *The Military in American Politics*. Chapter 5, "The Military, the Media, Politics and Public Opinion." New York: Harper & Row, 1973.

Cockburn, Andrew. "Covering Arms Control: A TWQ Roundtable." *Washington Quarterly* 5 (1982): 143–50.

——. "Graphic Evidence . . . of Nuclear Confusion." *Columbia Journalism Review*, May–June 1983, 38–41.

Cohen, Bernard C. "The Influence of Special-Interest Groups and Mass Media on Security Policy in the United States." In *Perspectives on American Foreign Policy: Selected Readings*, edited by Charles W. Kegley, Jr., and Eugene R. Wittkopf. New York: St. Martin's Press, 1983.

——. "Mass Communication and Foreign Policy." In *Domestic Sources of Foreign Policy*, edited by James N. Rosenau. New York: Free Press, 1967.

——. *The Press and Foreign Policy*. Princeton: Princeton University Press, 1963.

"Covering Nuclear Issues, Arms Control, and SDI." In *Between the Summits: a Conference Held at New York University, May 2, 1986*, edited by Robert Karl Manoff and Gerd Ruge. New York: Center for War, Peace and the News Media, 1988.

Cutler, Lloyd N. "Foreign Policy on Deadline." *Foreign Policy*, no. 56 (Fall 1984): 113–28.

Dalton, Gregory. *The Print Media and Arms Control Compliance*. Occasional Paper No. 1. Palo Alto: Global Outlook Institute, 1987.

Delauer, Richard D. "Shape Up: A Pentagon View of the Press." *Columbia Journalism Review*, Sept.–Oct. 1983, 17–20.

Desmond, Robert W. *The Press and World Affairs*. New York: D. Appleton-Century, 1938.

DeYoung, Karen. "Understanding U.S. Foreign Policy: The Role of the Press." *USA Today* [periodical], Jan. 1985, 66–69.

Diamond, Edwin, and George A. Gelish. "The Geneva Talks Are: (a) Hopeless (b) Promising (c) of Distant Concern." *TV Guide*, June 29, 1985, 26–31.

Dorman, William A. "The Media: Playing the Government's Game." In *Assessing the Nuclear Age*, edited by Len Ackland and Steven McGuire. Chicago: University of Chicago Press, 1986.

D'Souza, Dinesh. "TV News: The Politics of Social Climbing." *Policy Review*, Summer 1986, 24–31.

Dye, Thomas, Harmon Zeigler, and Robert Lichter. *American Politics in the Media Age*. Pacific Grove, Calif.: Brooks/Cole, 1992.

English, Robert, and Jonathan Halperin, eds. *The Other Side: How Soviets and Americans Perceive Each Other*. New Brunswick, N.J.: Transaction, 1987.

Epstein, Edward Jay. *News from Nowhere: Television and the News*. New York: Random House, 1973.

Ford, Gerald R. "Making Foreign Policy: How TV Influences a President's Decisions." *TV Guide*, Sept. 19, 1981, 5–8.

Franck, Thomas M., and Edward Weisband, eds. *Secrecy and Foreign Policy*. New York: Oxford University Press, 1974.

Friel, Howard. "Covert Propaganda in *Time* and *Newsweek*." *Covert Action Information Bulletin*, Spring 1984, 14–23.

Gamson, William A. "Reframing the Debate." *Nuclear Times*, July–Aug. 1987, 27–30.

Gans, Herbert. *Deciding What's News*. New York: Pantheon Books, 1979.

Garneau, George. "President Reagan and Disinformation." *Editor and Publisher*, Oct. 24, 1987, 9–10.

Geylin, Philip L. "Managing the Media." *Fletcher Forum of World Affairs* 13 (Winter 1989): 19–23.

Gilmore, Dan F. "Military and the Media." *Editor and Publisher*, Sept. 13, 1986, 11–12.

Gitlin, Todd. *The Whole World Is Watching*. Berkeley: University of California Press, 1980.

Goren, Dina. "The News and Foreign Policy: An Examination of the Impact of the News Media on the Making of Foreign Policy." *Research in Social Movements, Conflicts and Change* 3 (1980): 119–41.

Gottschalk, Jack A. " 'Consistent with Security' . . . A History of American Military Press Censorship." *Communication and the Law* 5 (1983): 35–52.

Graber, Doris. *Mass Media and American Politics*. 3d ed. Washington, D.C.: Congressional Quarterly Press, 1989.

Grossman, Michael B., and Francis E. Rourke. "The Media and the Presidency: An Exchange Analysis." *Political Science Quarterly* 91 (1976): 455–70.

Habeeb, William Mark. *Power and Tactics in International Negotiation*. Baltimore: Johns Hopkins University Press, 1988.

Haig, Alexander M. "TV Can Derail Diplomacy." *TV Guide*, Mar. 9, 1985, 4–8.

Hallin, Daniel C. "The Myth of the Adversary Press." *Quill*, Nov. 1983, 30–36.

Halperin, Morton H. "Focus On: Freedom of Information and National Security." *Journal of Peace Research* 20 (1983): 1–4.

——. "Secrecy and National Security." *Bulletin of Atomic Scientists*, Aug. 1985, 114–17.

Heise, Juergen Arthur. *Minimum Disclosure: How the Pentagon Manipulates the News*. New York: Norton, 1979.

Herman, Edward S., and Norm Chomsky. *Manufacturing Consent.* New York: Pantheon, 1988.

Hess, Stephen. "The Golden Triangle: Press Relations at the White House, State Department, and Department of Defense." In *War Peace and the News Media, a Conference Held at New York University, March 18–19, 1983,* edited by David M. Rubin and Ann Marie Cunningham. New York: Center for War, Peace and the News Media, 1987.

———. *The Washington Reporters.* Washington, D.C.: Brookings Institute. 1981.

———. *The Government-Press Connection.* Washington, D.C.: Brookings Institute, 1984.

Hinckley, Ronald H. *People, Polls, and Policy-Makers.* New York: Lexington Books, 1992.

Hofstetter, C. R., and D. W. Moore. "Watching TV News and Supporting the Military." *Armed Forces and Society* 5 (1979): 261–69.

Ikle, Fred Charles. *How Nations Negotiate.* New York: Harper & Row, 1964.

Irvine, Reed. "Amateur Newsmen Showed Up Pros at Geneva." *Human Events,* No. 8 (Dec. 7, 1985).

Iyengar, Shanto, Mark Peters, and Donald R. Kinder. "Experimental Demonstrations of the 'Not-So-Minimal' Political Consequences of Television News Programs." *Mass Communication Review Yearbook,* Vol. 4. Beverly Hills: Sage, 1983.

Joyce, Alisa. "Gunning for Respect in the Pentagon Press Corps." *In These Times,* May 13–19, 1987, 12–13.

Kampelman, Max M. "Congress, the Media, and the President." *Academy of Political Science Proceedings* 32, no. 1 (1975): 89–97.

———. *Entering New Worlds: The Memoirs of a Private Man in Public Life.* New York: Harper Collins, 1991.

———. "Negotiating with the Soviet Union." *World Affairs* 148 (Spring 1986): 199–203.

Katz, Elihu, Hanna Adona, and Pnina Parness. "Remembering the News: What the Picture Adds to Recall." *Journalism Quarterly* 54 (Summer 1977): 231–39.

Kegley, Charles, and Eugene R. Wittkopf. *American Foreign Policy: Pattern and Process.* 3d ed. New York: St. Martin's Press, 1987.

Kernell, Samuel. *Going Public: New Strategies of Presidential Leadership.* Washington, D.C.: Congressional Quarterly Press, 1986.

Kirkhorn, Michael J. "Nuclear Arms Reporting: Not with a Bang, but a Whisper." *Quill,* July–Aug. 1983, 10–16.

Krepon, Michael. "Arms Control Play-by-Play." *Bulletin of Atomic Scientists*, Mar. 1988, 5–6.

———. "The PR Administration." *Bulletin of Atomic Scientists*, Nov. 1986, 6–7.

Krippendorff, Klaus. *Content Analysis: An Introduction to Its Methodology*. Beverly Hills: Sage, 1980.

Kwitny, Jonathan. *Endless Enemies: The Making of an Unfriendly World*. Chapter 22, "Lies: The Government and the Press." New York: Congdon and Weed, 1984.

Lang, Gladys Engel, and Kurt Lang. *The Battle for Public Opinion: The President, the Press, and the Polls During Watergate*. New York: Columbia University Press, 1983.

Ledeen, Michael. "Public Opinion, Press Opinion, and Foreign Policy." *Public Opinion*, Aug.–Sept. 1984, 5–7.

Le Duc, Don R. "Television Coverage of NATO Affairs." *Journal of Broadcasting* 24 (1980): 449–65.

Lee, Richard W., ed. *Politics and the Press*. Washington, D.C.: Acropolis Books, 1970.

Lefever, Ernest W. "The Prestige Press, Foreign Policy and American Survival." *Orbis* 20 (1976): 207–25.

———. *TV and National Defense: An Analysis of CBS News, 1972–1973*. Boston: Institute for American Strategy Press, 1974.

Lichter, Robert S., Linda S. Lichter, and Stanley Rothman. *Watching America*. New York: Prentice-Hall, 1991.

Lichter, Robert S., and Stanley Rothman. "Media and Business Elites." *Public Opinion*, Oct.–Nov. 1981, 42.

Lichter, Robert S., Stanley Rothman, and Linda S. Lichter. *The Media Elite*. Bethesda, Md.: Adler & Adler, 1986.

Linsky, Martin. *Impact: How the Press Affects Federal Policy Making*. New York: Norton, 1986.

Lovell, John P. "The Idiom of National Security." *Journal of Political and Military Sociology* 11 (1983): 35–51.

Mackuen, Michael Bruce, and Steven Lane Coombs. *More Than the News: Media Power in Public Affairs*. Beverly Hills: Sage, 1981.

Madison, Christopher. "State Department Press Briefings Losing Value as Key Source of Diplomatic News." *National Journal*, Nov. 9, 1985, 2531–34.

Manning, Robert J. "Journalism and Foreign Affairs." In *Responsibility of the Press*, edited by Gerald Gross. New York: Simon and Schuster, 1966.

Manoff, Robert Karl. "Anatomy of a Leak." *Deadline*, Mar.–Apr. 1986, 6–8.

——. "Covering the Bomb: Press and State in the Shadow of Nuclear War." In *War, Peace and the News Media, a Conference Held at New York University, March 18–19, 1983*, edited by David M. Rubin and Ann-Marie Cunningham. New York: Center for War, Peace and the News Media, 1987.

——. *Narrative Strategy and Nuclear News*. Occasional Paper No. 1. New York: Center for War, Peace and the News Media, 1987.

——. "Reporting the Nuclear News in an Era of U.S.-Soviet Accord." *Deadline*, July–Aug. 1988, 1–2ff.

——. "What Is the Real Message That Rocky and Dan Rather Send?" *Deadline*, May–June 1986, 8–9.

——. "Who Speaks and How: Some Notes on Nuclear Discourse." In *A Proxy for Knowledge: The News Media as Agents for Arms Control and Verification*, edited by Peter A. Bruck. Ottawa, Canada: Carleton International Proceedings, 1988.

Marder, Murray. "Journalism's Nuclear Burden." *Nieman Reports*, Spring 1985, 5–7.

Marro, Anthony. "When the Government Tells Lies." *Columbia Journalism Review*, Mar.–Apr. 1985, 29–41.

Massing, Michael L. *Euromissiles and the Press*. Occasional Paper No. 2. New York: Center for War, Peace, and the News Media, 1987.

Mautner-Markhof, Frances, ed. *Processes of International Negotiations*. Boulder: Westview Press, 1989.

Mazza, Patrick. "Pumping for Peace." *Nuclear Times*, Sept.–Oct. 1987, 17–19.

McCombs, Maxwell E., and Donald Shaw. "The Agenda-Setting Function of the Mass Media." *Public Opinion Quarterly* 36 (1972): 176–87.

——. "The Agenda-Setting Function of the Press." In *Media Power in Politics*, edited by Doris Graber. Washington, D.C.: Congressional Quarterly Press, 1984.

——. *Emergence of American Political Issues: The Agenda Setting Function of the Press*. St. Paul: West, 1977.

McHenry, R. W., ed. *Media and Defense: Areas of Stress*. Mclean, Va.: National Concerns, 1982.

"Medium-Range Missiles and the Media: Roundup on Press Coverage of INF." Analyses by John Steinbruner, Edward Luttwak, Patricia Schroeder, Paul Warnke, General Frederick Kroesen, Randall Forsberg, and Chalmers Hardenbergh. *Deadline*, July–Aug. 1987, 3–5.

Mehan, Hugh, and James M. Skelly. "Mum's the Word at Geneva Summit." *Broadcasting*, Nov. 25, 1985, 34–35.

——. "1988–2001: The Treaty Makes News." *Deadline*, July–Aug. 1988, 3–5.

The Military and the Media. Essays on Strategy and Diplomacy, No. 2. Claremont, Calif.: Keck Center for International Strategic Studies, Claremont McKenna College, 1984.

"Military-Media Relations." *Editor and Publisher*, Nov. 21, 1987, 15ff.

Nash, Steve. "Coverage of Arms Race Stirs Debate in N.Y." *Editor and Publisher*, Mar. 26, 1983, 44.

Nincic, Miroslav. *United States Foreign Policy: Choices and Trade-offs*. Washington, D.C.: Congressional Quarterly, 1988.

Nitze, Paul H. *From Hiroshima to Glasnost: At the Center of Decision—A Memoir*, New York: Grove Weidenfeld, 1989.

O'Heffernan, Patrick. *Mass Media and American Foreign Policy: Insider Perspectives on Global Journalism and the Foreign Policy Process*. Norwood, N.J.: Ablex, 1991.

Oldendick, Robert W., and Barbara Ann Bardes. "Mass Media and Elite Foreign Policy Opinions." *Public Opinion Quarterly* 46 (1982): 368–82.

Ornstein, Norman, Andrew Kohut, and Larry McCarthy. *The People, the Press, and Politics*. Reading, Mass.: Addison-Wesley, 1988.

Parenti, Michael. *Inventing Reality: The Politics of the Mass Media*. New York: St. Martin's Press, 1986.

Philips, Kevin. "Media Elite's Influence on Foreign Policy." *TV Guide*, Aug. 23, 1975, A3–A11.

Pringle, Peter. "Hand-Me-Down Scoop." *New Republic*, Mar. 25, 1985, 6–8.

Pugh, Tom. "Geneva 'Background.'" *Nation*, Mar. 23, 1985, 324–25.

Rachlin, Allan. *News as Hegemonic Reality: American Political Culture and the Framing of News Accounts*. New York: Praeger, 1988.

Rangarajan, L. N. *The Limitation of Conflict: A Theory of Bargaining and Negotiation*. New York: St. Martin's Press, 1985.

Ranney, Austin. *Channels of Power: The Impact of Television in American Politics*. New York: Basic Books, 1983.

Reed, Fred. "'Can Our Public Affairs Officer Help?' How the Military Keeps the Press in the Dark." *Washington Monthly*, Oct. 1984, 20–26.

Reilly, John. *American Public Opinion and U.S. Foreign Policy*. Chicago: Chicago Council on Foreign Relations, 1987.

Reston, James. *The Artillery of the Press*. New York: Harper & Row, 1966.

——. "The Press, the President, and Foreign Policy." *In Mass Media and*

Communication, edited by Charles S. Steinburg. New York: Harper & Row, 1972.

Rice, Michael, and James A. Cooney. *Reporting U.S.-European Relations*. New York: Pergamon, 1982.

Robinson, Michael J., and Maura E. Clancey. "King of the Hill." *Washington Journalism Review*, July–Aug. 1983, 46–48.

——. "A 98-Pound Weakling?" *Washingtonian*, Nov. 1983, 73–81.

Robinson, Michael J., and Margaret A. Sheehan. *Over the Wire and on TV: CBS and UPI in Campaign '80*. New York: Russell Sage Foundation, 1983.

Rosen, Jay. *Democracy Overwhelmed: Press and Public in the Nuclear Age*. Occasional Paper No. 4. New York: Center for War, Peace, and the News Media, 1988.

——. "Public Knowledge/Private Ignorance." *Deadline*, Jan.–Feb. 1987, 1–4.

——. "Suppose They Held a Summit and No Reporters Came." *Deadline*, Mar.–Apr. 1986, 9–12.

——. "What We Know About Arms Race Is More Than a Matter of Opinion." *Deadline*, May–June 1986, 1–2.

Rubin, David M. "INF Inspections: U.S. and U.S.S.R. Quietly Limit Press Access." *Deadline*, Sept.–Oct. 1988, 3–4ff.

——. "A Range of Opinion as Narrow as Scarlett O'Hara's Waist." *Deadline*, May–June 1986, 2–3.

——. "Television Signs an INF Pact." *Deadline*, Nov.–Dec. 1987, 10–11.

——. "Tracking the Arms Control Story: What's New? What's True?" *Deadline*, May–June 1987, 3ff.

——. "Why Not Declare the New York Times a Nuclear Proliferation Zone?" *Deadline*, May–June 1986, 2–3.

Rubin, Richard L. *Press, Party, and Presidency*. New York: Norton, 1981.

Sandman, Peter M., David M. Rubin, and David B. Sachsman. *Media: An Introductory Analysis of American Mass Communications*. Englewood Cliffs, N.J.: Prentice-Hall, 1982.

Sarskesian, Sam C. "Soldiers, Scholars, and the Media." *Parameters*, Sept. 1987, 77–87.

Schlitz, Timothy, Lee Sigelman, and Robert Neal. "Perspectives of Managing Editors on Coverage of Foreign Policy News." *Journalism Quarterly* 50 (1973): 716–21.

Schneider, William. "Television's Gift to the Policymaker." *Chronicle of International Communication*, May 1982, 6–7.

Serfaty, Simon, ed. *The Media and Foreign Policy.* New York: St. Martin's Press, 1991.

Shapley, Deborah. "The Media and National Security." *Daedalus* 111 (1982): 199–209.

Sigal, Leon V. *Reporters and Officials: The Organization and Politics of Newsmaking.* Lexington, Mass.: D. C. Heath, 1973.

"Soviet Propaganda and U.S. Press." *Editor and Publisher,* Nov. 2, 1985, 8.

Taishoff, S. "Tricky Treaty: Covering the Quest for Arms Control." *Media Monitor,* Nov. 1987, 1–4.

———. "TV, Too, Has a Role in the Drive for Detente." *Advertising Age,* Mar. 4, 1985, 50.

Talbott, Strobe. *Deadly Gambits.* New York: Knopf, 1984.

Thakur, Ramesh, ed. *International Conflict Resolution.* Boulder: Westview Press, 1988.

"There Aren't Any Poor Questions, Only Poor Answers." Excerpts from a conference on press coverage of the Geneva summit, nuclear arms, and Soviet and American society held in New York on May 2, 1986. *Deadline,* July–Aug. 1986, 7–9.

Tyson, James L. *Target America: The Influence of Communist Propaganda on U.S. Media.* Chicago: Regnery Gateway, 1982.

———. "Target America: The Influence of Soviet Propaganda on U.S. Media. *Strategic Review,* Winter 1982, 70–73.

Walker, Jack L. "Setting the Agenda in the U.S. Senate: A Theory of Problem Selection." *British Journal of Political Science* 7 (1977): 423–45.

Wallach, John P. " 'I'll Give It to You on Background': State Breakfasts." *Washington Quarterly* 5 (1982): 53–66.

Weaver, Davis H., Doris A. Graber, Maxwell E. McCombs, and Eyal H. Chaim. *Media Agenda-Setting in a Presidential Election: Issues, Images, and Interest.* New York: Praeger, 1981.

Wines, Michael. "Should Reporters Keep State Secrets?" *Washington Journalism Review,* Nov. 1986, 32–37.

Wise, David. *The Politics of Lying: Government Deception, Secrecy, and Power.* New York: Random House, 1973.

Zartman, William I., and Maureen R. Berman. *The Practical Negotiator.* New Haven: Yale University Press, 1982.

Index

In this index an "f" after a number indicates a separate reference on the next page, and an "ff" indicates separate references on the next two pages. A continuous discussion over two or more pages is indicated by a span of page numbers, e.g., "57–59." *Passim* is used for a cluster of references in close but not consecutive sequence.

Library of Congress Cataloging-in-Publication Data
Genest, Marc A.
    Negotiating in the public eye : the impact of the press on the intermediate-range nuclear force negotiations / Marc A. Genest
        p. cm.
    Includes bibliographical references and index.
    ISBN 0-8047-2439-3 (acid-free-paper)
    1. Soviet Union. Treaties, etc. United States, 1987 Dec. 8. 2. Nuclear arms control—United States. 3. Nuclear arms control—Soviet Union. 4. Intermediate-range ballistic missiles. 5. Europe—Defenses. 6. North Atlantic Treaty Organization. 7. Mass media—Influence.
JX1974.7.G4286 1995
327.1'74'0947—dc20   94-28866
CIP
⊗ This book is printed on acid-free, recycled paper.